London's archaeological secrets

A world city revealed

edited by Chris Thomas

with Andy Chopping and Tracy Wellman

Yale University Press
New Haven and London

in association with the
Museum of London Archaeology Service

MUSEUM OF LONDON
Archaeology Service

Printed in the United Kingdom.

Library of Congress Control Number: 2002100709

ISBN 0-300-09516-3 (cloth : alk. paper)
ISBN 0-300-09517-1 (paper : alk. paper)

A catalogue record for this book is available from the British Library

The paper in this book meets the guidelines for permanence and durability of the Committee
on Production Guidelines for Book Longevity of the Council on Library Resources.

10 9 8 7 6 5 4 3 2 1

Front cover Sir Christopher Wren's church St Dunstan
in the East, in the City of London
Back cover An early Roman mosaic floor; an enamelled
medieval glass beaker; 13th-century keys from the
monastery of St Mary Spital; late 16th-century watering
cans found in a well

Contents

London's
archaeological secrets

Introduction

Foreword

by Peter Hinton, Director, Institute of Field Archaeologists

Archaeology is often thought of as the study of dry and dusty objects by dry and dusty people – broken bones and potsherds painstakingly examined by an academic elite far removed from real life.

This is not how archaeology is today. It is a discipline of great popular interest, reaching almost all sectors of society through books, museums, schools and television. There are good reasons for this.

Archaeology gives us a link to the past, and sometimes a very different past. It digs deeper for truths not found in history books and tells us of the lives of ordinary people, not just kings and queens. It does not look only at the great buildings and monuments of the tourist trail, but also at ordinary houses, at rubbish, sewage and humble graves. By doing so it provides us with a

sense of place, of identity and of belonging. It shows us that the problems of today (whether of housing a city's population, providing amenities, freeing up the thoroughfares, combating crime or helping different social and ethnic groups to live together) are not new – and, by explaining how and where we fit in a long story, perhaps gives a better understanding of how to tackle those problems.

This, then, is not a book about things, but about people. First of all it is about the people of the past, the wave upon wave of immigrant populations that have come to London to make it the world city it is today. It tells us about how they lived, about the tensions between them and how they made a fortune or scraped a living, about what they believed in and what they feared, what they ate, what they wore,

how they enjoyed themselves and how they died.

Secondly, this book tells us about the work of London's archaeologists. It examines their lives in less intimate detail than those of the past populations, but as you read this book you will get an impression of a new and dedicated profession, working in a business-like fashion to provide new understandings of a complex metropolis. This book is a tribute to their hard work, poorly rewarded and often undertaken in adversity, but inspired by a desire to reveal London's archaeological secrets to those that live there, visit or just want to learn more about this capital city. It is also a tribute to the many generations of people who made modern London the place it is to live in, work in, visit or admire from afar.

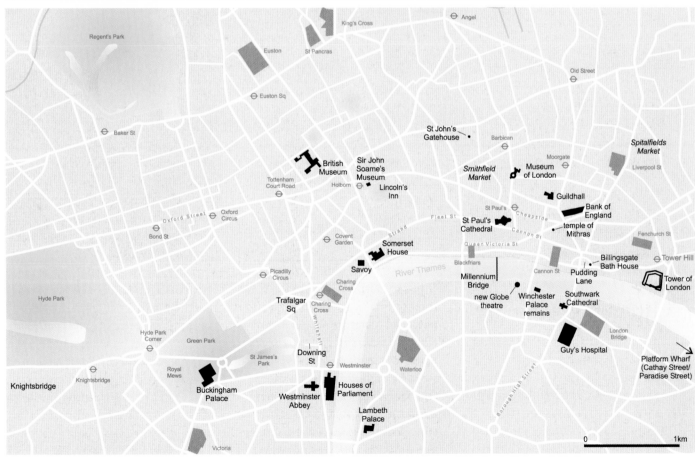

Modern London

Left Places within the Greater London area mentioned in the text; **Below** Places mentioned in the text and some of the places one can visit

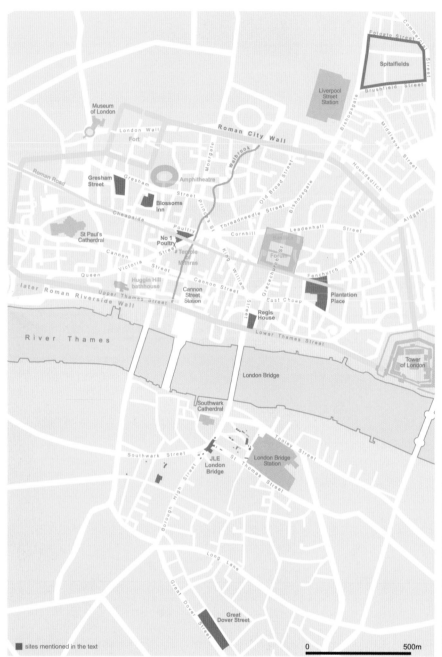

sites mentioned in the text

0   500m

Above left Map showing major features within Roman London, and locating some of the major sites mentioned in the text; **Above top** Recording part of the amphitheatre wall; **Above** The beautifully preserved mosiac floor found on the site at Gresham Street

Roman London

The Roman City was founded on the north bank of the Thames in what we now know as the City of London, popularly called the Square Mile. In the centre lay the forum and in the north-west corner the fort and the amphitheatre. The Roman city soon acquired its own suburb on the south side of the river in Southwark which was based around the other end of London Bridge.

Right Map showing medieval London, with its street pattern very similar to that of today. The monastic precincts covered vast areas around the city. Some of the major sites mentioned in the text are also shown; **Below** Recording a chalk garderobe (toilet) on the moatside wall of the medieval manor house at Low Hall, Walthamstow

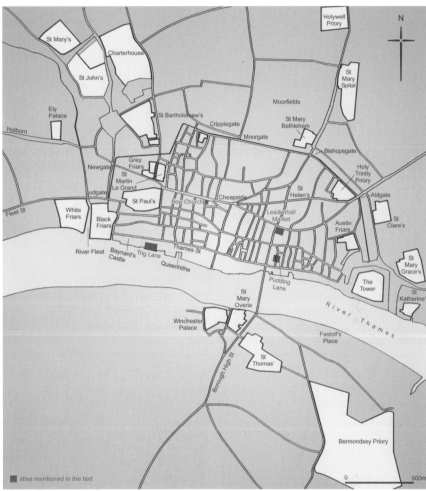

Medieval London

The medieval city originally had much the same boundaries as its Roman predecessor with all the people crammed inside the city walls and in Southwark. This is why so many of London's monasteries were founded outside of the walls in what were then open fields. Suburbs developed in the medieval period alongside the roads but it wasn't until the seventeenth century that London really began to expand beyond its walled city.

Excavating the 17th-century brick cellar of a Jacobean house

The history of London's archaeology

A Museum archaeologist carefully cleaning the remains of a decorative mosaic floor discovered almost 6 m below today's ground surface on the site of 1 Poultry in the City

Archaeology in London

How many of us, when we walk down London's streets, think about the thousands of years of history buried beneath our feet? We may look up at the mixture of buildings old and new, but rarely do we stop to consider how much of our knowledge of London's past comes from the archaeological remains buried beneath the ground.

The Roman and medieval City wall at Tower Hill still stands up to 11 m high; the statue of a Roman emperor was made in the 19th century

Left The Museum of London's Archaeological Archive and Research Centre is home to 20% of the whole of England's archaeological archive, accessibly stored on over 11 km of shelving and including 250,000 individually registered finds and 120,000 boxes of general finds such as pottery and bone; **Below** An archaeologist records a Roman defensive ditch – the distinctions within the section indicate different phases of activity

2 A stylised cross-section through a London street, demonstrating that the present jumble of historic and modern buildings sits on an artificial mound of previous occupation and destruction debris accumulated through the 2000 years of the city's history

Right The site of Lion Plaza in the heart of London's financial district. In spite of the fact that the City has been extensively developed and redeveloped, the majority of construction sites still offer archaeologists the opportunity to glimpse aspects of the lives of earlier citizens 3

The physical evidence for London's past has been studied for hundreds of years, but it has only been systematically investigated by professional organisations, largely based at the Museum of London, since the early 1970s. 1 This book celebrates that period of professional full-time archaeological study in London, and the 25th anniversary of the Museum of London. In addition it illustrates many of the great archaeological discoveries made in the previous 200 years by other antiquarians and archaeologists, who began the work of piecing together a picture of London's past and its people.

London has been an important site for almost 2000 years, and there is abundant evidence of the prehistoric peoples who lived in the region for many thousands of years before that. Today, London is still centred around the historic core of the Roman and medieval City, with its suburb of Southwark on the south bank of the River Thames and the political capital of Westminster a mile or so upstream. Outside these areas once

lay open fields interspersed with towns and villages, prehistoric camps, Roman cemeteries, monasteries, medieval manor houses and various other kinds of sites – all now buried beneath the vast urban sprawl of the modern city.

Because London has been inhabited for so long, many of its archaeological treasures lie deep below the ground as successive generations have built on top of previous structures. Over the centuries this has created a 'layer-cake' of archaeological deposits, 2 sometimes as much as 7 m deep, particularly close to the river. The outer edges of London often have a less intensive history of occupation and the 'layer-cake' is that much shallower, but even then there may be 4 m or more of history beneath the modern ground. Most of the archaeological discoveries illustrated in this book were found during redevelopment for new offices, housing, shops, schools, hospitals and transport systems, built to sustain modern London. 3

Naturally, a book such as this can only scratch the surface of the huge amount of information recovered over the years. It explores some of the most exciting archaeological discoveries in London and explains what they can tell us about the people who made the city we know today. Many of London's archaeological monuments 4 can still be visited, as shown on the maps, but numerous other past glories of the city exist now only as finds in boxes, or photographs in cabinets and records on pieces of paper. 5 The Museum of London Archaeology Service has embarked on a massive programme of publishing academic and popular books on many of these findings, covering them in much more detail. Here we describe and illustrate just some of the remarkable discoveries which have been made in one of the world's most important capital cities, uncovering some of its secrets and shedding light on London's rich and varied past.

An annotated drawing by William Stukeley made on May Day 1725, near Kenwood. Stukeley describes his subject as 'the tumulus of some antient Brittish king before Christianity'

Antiquarian interest in the past led to the illustrated recording of some finds, even if they were not fully understood; **Above** An assortment of Roman and medieval artefacts from the City; **Below** A humorous sketch entitled 'Excavation of a barrow, 1844', from the *Gentleman's Magazine*, 1852

Antiquarian recording

While archaeology has been recognised as a science only since the nineteenth century and as a profession in the much more recent past, people have been recording their physical history for a great deal longer.

Charles Roach Smith's collection of London antiquities on display in 1850

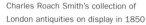

Left One of the detailed watercolours made by architect Henry Hodge of parts of the Roman basilica and medieval Leadenhall, uncovered at Leadenhall Street in the 1880s; **Above** For the past 200 years archaeologists have been using the opportunities provided by redevelopment to understand the constructions of the past, as illustrated here by the discovery during the rebuilding of old London Bridge in 1832 of an earlier chapel undercroft

Left An estimated 50,000 people came to see the Bucklersbury mosaic over the space of three days in 1869

In his *Survey of London,* John Stow described much of the city in the latter part of the sixteenth century, including the extraordinary Roman burials that were found in Spitalfields. Sir Christopher Wren, the architect of St Paul's Cathedral, recorded a Roman road to the south of Cheapside when he rebuilt Bow Church in the late seventeenth century, and in the eighteenth century William Stukeley, ① an early antiquarian, made a study of the belfry of Westminster Abbey, a detached bell-tower, prior to its demolition. During the latter part of the eighteenth century and the early years of the nineteenth, much work was done on documenting parts of the medieval and later buildings in the Palace of Westminster. Antiquarians such as J. T. Smith and W. Capon described in detail many of the buildings, while others copied some of the magnificent medieval wall paintings revealed when later plaster was removed. Had it not been for such scholars, an enormous amount of information would have been lost when the Palace was almost totally destroyed by fire in 1834.

On the whole, these early antiquarians were interested in recording structures that still survived above ground. Later, in the course of the nineteenth century, more artefacts and archaeological sites were recovered

from beneath the city's streets. One of the most famous discoveries was the Bucklersbury Pavement, a magnificent Roman mosaic floor. ② Thousands flocked to see this when it was found in 1869 during the building of Queen Victoria Street. It probably dates to the third century AD and obviously belonged to a very fine building, but since little else was recorded we cannot say much about the structure it embellished. Another remarkable find was the Roman boat ③ uncovered in the early twentieth century during the construction of the new headquarters of the London County Council, opposite the Houses of Parliament.

The twentieth century saw the beginnings of new techniques of archaeological recording in London and elsewhere, with great care taken to document the structures and their associated layers of soil, as well as the finds that came from them. W. H. St John Hope, an archaeologist who excavated and described many of the famous monasteries in Britain, recorded parts of St John's Clerkenwell, including its round nave. The first archaeologist at the Guildhall Museum was Frank Lambert, who began work there in 1907. Other well-known archaeologists from the era before the Second World War include Gerald Dunning and Frank Cottrill, who worked for the Society of Antiquaries.

Cottrill recorded parts of the church and cloister at St Mary Spital, the granary and a bridge at Westminster Abbey, and the Roman City wall on Tower Hill.

These pioneering archaeologists, working under great pressure and with few resources, laid the foundations for the professionals of the future. A concerted approach to archaeological recording in London was still lacking, however, and some significant sites, where large quantities of finds were recovered, were inadequately recorded, such as the excavation at the Bank of England during the years 1926–36.

A display at the old Guildhall Museum of artefacts found in 1870 during building work in Queen Victoria Street

Above Looking south down Walbrook on the morning of 11 May 1941 after an attack on London which left 1436 killed, 1800 seriously injured, 8000 streets impassable and 2154 fires requiring attendance. This awful destruction was to lead to the discovery of the Temple of Mithras beneath the remains of the building on the right

Post-war London

The terrible destruction of the Second World War provided unparalleled opportunities to investigate large areas of London which had been severely damaged during the Blitz.

Archaeologists working in the ruins of London's buildings ① discovered treasures from many periods of the city's past. Professor W. F. Grimes, working under the auspices of the Roman and Medieval London Excavation Council, was especially active, and several of his findings feature in later chapters of this book. His most famous excavation was at the Temple of Mithras, on the site now occupied by Bucklersbury House, in 1952. Here he found a well-preserved third- and fourth-century Roman temple ② from which he recovered, among many other artefacts, the head of a statue of the god Mithras. ③ Queues of people turned up to see it, ④ as they had done in the previous century for the Bucklersbury Pavement, found only a few metres away. Grimes also investigated

the bombed-out remains of the Barbican, where he excavated large areas of the Roman fort, ⑤ as well as medieval and later churches. His work on the fort proved to be fundamental to our understanding of both the layout and the development of Roman London. Grimes' investigation of St Bride's Church in Fleet Street demonstrated that an enormous amount could be learnt by excavating the remains of ruined medieval parish churches, previously considered not worthy of archaeological study because so many others still stood.

Grimes extended his work beyond the Roman and medieval walled city, digging on the site of Bermondsey Abbey, where he found part of the east end of the church, and at the London Charterhouse ⑥ near

Above 'To the temple of Mithras' – a drawing by Fougasse provides a perfect and ironic view of the massive public interest in the discovery

Smithfield Market. This was the site of a Carthusian monastery, a mansion once owned by the Dukes of Norfolk, a famous school and a retirement home for elderly men which was badly bombed during the war. Rebuilding work allowed excavations to be carried out which uncovered the site of the old church and the tomb of the founder, Sir Walter Manny, still clutching a papal bulla (edict) in his hand. A similar strategy of excavations on bomb sites, but on a much smaller scale, was carried out in Southwark by Kathleen Kenyon for the Surrey Archaeological Society, beginning in 1945.

In the 1950s, while Grimes continued his research excavations, the Guildhall Museum's archaeologist, Ivor Noel-Hume, **7** excavated what he could of sites that were rapidly being destroyed by redevelopment. From the late 1950s until the formation of the Department of Urban Archaeology in 1973, archaeological coverage in the City of London was limited to the efforts of only a handful of archaeologists, including in particular Peter Marsden, who worked for the Guildhall Museum. The pace of redevelopment meant that such a limited number of archaeologists could not possibly record all that was being destroyed, and the 1960s was a decade of loss for our archaeological heritage. In spite of some setbacks, important remains were recorded, in particular the Roman forum, the Roman bath-houses of Huggin Hill **8** and Billingsgate, and on the site of what was thought to be the Roman Governor's Palace at Cannon Street.

Queen Elizabeth the Queen Mother being shown a model of the new Museum of London which opened in 1975

Archaeologists in London in the 1970s worked in an environment very different from that of today, unconcerned with issues of sun damage, unconfined by health and safety regulations insisting on safety boots and hard hats, and usually enjoying sole occupancy of a building site. **Above left** One of the earliest sites in London where the medieval waterfront was found; **Above** A 2nd-century Roman mosaic floor discovered in remarkable condition at Milk Street in the City

Scientific dating systems available to the modern archaeologist include archaeomagnetic dating; samples – in this case from a Saxon bread oven – are taken back to the laboratory for analysis

Professional archaeology

Archaeology in London is now highly organised and professional, playing a key role in safeguarding the city's past.

It was only at the end of 1973 that the Department of Urban Archaeology (DUA) was formed, funded by central government and with responsibility for the archaeology of the City of London. As a guide the DUA used 'The future of London's past', an outline of the state of knowledge of London's archaeology at the time, with recommendations on how best to look after it.

Archaeologists had already identified some of the most potentially rewarding areas for investigation, in particular along the riverfront. Initially excavations found extensive and well-preserved medieval waterfronts. ① Later archaeologists discovered not only superb remains of the

Roman waterfronts, but also what has been interpreted as part of the Roman London Bridge, in the vicinity of Pudding Lane. Other areas of interest included the City walls, the Roman forum, Baynard's Castle, Bridewell Palace, a possible Roman fort at Aldgate, Roman streets in the area of Cannon Street, six medieval religious houses, Leadenhall and the possible site of the Roman Governor's Palace. And many other areas unexpectedly proved to be equally exciting, such as the Guildhall, with the discovery of the Roman amphitheatre and medieval remains. The more archaeologists excavated, the more they confounded the unduly pessimistic predictions of what might survive beneath London's modern buildings. ②

By 1978 the DUA was starting to try to persuade developers that they should pay for the excavations on their building sites, and by 1980 funding began to include basic processing of the data and the finds, as well as cataloguing, report writing and archiving.

The archaeological groups who covered areas outside the city were mostly established by county archaeological societies. The Surrey Archaeological Society helped set up the Southwark Archaeological Excavation Committee (SAEC) in 1962, which later became SLAEC when they extended their work to Lambeth in 1975, and the South-West London Archaeological Unit in 1974. The West London Archaeological Unit was formed in the early 1960s, beginning their work in Brentford, mainly on prehistoric sites. The London and Middlesex Archaeological Society (LAMAS) set up the Inner London Archaeological Unit to cover north London around the City from Tower Hamlets in the east to Hammersmith in the west. North-east London, in the area which had historically been Essex, was covered by the Passmore Edwards Museum, and the Kent Archaeological Rescue Service carried out work in parts of south-east London.

In 1983 the four archaeology units were amalgamated in the Museum of London to form the Department of Greater London Archaeology (DGLA), though they continued to operate as sections within the DGLA until 1991, when the DUA and the DGLA were amalgamated as the Museum of London Archaeology Service (MoLAS). In addition to MoLAS, a number of other archaeological units now work in London as a result of the system of competitive tendering introduced in the early 1990s. These include AOC Archaeology, Wessex Archaeology, Oxford Archaeology and Pre-Construct Archaeology.

Archaeological practice has changed enormously over recent years, with the introduction of health and safety measures and the increasingly tight schedules allowed for the archaeologists to excavate as the value of redevelopments rose. Important advances in recording methods were made, which were standardised and published, and are now used by other archaeologists all around the world.

Today's London archaeologist may be a well-qualified and skilled excavator, finds recorder, environmental specialist, project manager, author, illustrator, surveyor or photographer. Working with other professionals in development, construction, surveying, tourism and education, archaeologists are part of multi-disciplinary teams, joining together to protect, investigate and share with others the excitement of London's past.

Below With the need to incorporate archaeology smoothly into the redevelopment process archaeologists are frequently required to work alongside demolition and construction companies, as here, below Borough High Street during the construction of the Jubilee tube line

Below The analysis of soils and sediments is one example of the way in which laboratory science is now an integral part of archaeological work

Keyhole glimpses into London's archaeology can be provided by deep shaft excavations or by mile after mile of shallow trenching running across the countryside, for the installation of a new road or pipe line. **Above top** This deep shaft a mere 4 m wide – with the tops of two Roman wooden wells just visible – was part of London Underground's Jubilee Line Extension project; **Above** Archaeologists followed the installation of this pipe line across Hampstead Heath for British Gas

London's landscape and topography

Right Looking northwest across the Thames before the foundation of London. Until comparatively recently the low-lying landscape south of the Thames was a series of islands; **Below right** The banks of the Thames and its low sandy islands would have offered good locations for fishing

London before London

London lies in a large, shallow, bowl-like area formed by the Thames Valley, and provided an excellent environment for prehistoric hunters and gatherers.

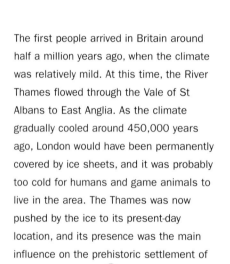

Above Reconstructed scene at Swanscombe around 350,000 years ago; **Below** The Swanscombe skull. The three conjoining fragments of this skull were found on three separate occasions, in 1935, 1936 and 1955

The first people arrived in Britain around half a million years ago, when the climate was relatively mild. At this time, the River Thames flowed through the Vale of St Albans to East Anglia. As the climate gradually cooled around 450,000 years ago, London would have been permanently covered by ice sheets, and it was probably too cold for humans and game animals to live in the area. The Thames was now pushed by the ice to its present-day location, and its presence was the main influence on the prehistoric settlement of the London region. ①

Then, around 400,000 to 300,000 years ago, the climate became warmer and people began to move back into Britain. The earliest evidence we have for humans in the London region is in the form of their flint tools, known as handaxes. These have been found in gravel terraces in Hillingdon and at Swanscombe, ② a gravel terrace close to the Thames, possibly dating as far back as 400,000 years. The humans that used these multi-purpose cutting and chopping tools were members of the species

Homo erectus ('upright man'). A skull ③ found at Swanscombe is possibly a quarter of a million years old – the earliest human remains found so far in Britain.

Around 120,000 years ago the climate was a few degrees warmer than today and the sea level was slightly higher. Britain was cut off from the continent of Europe for the first time, and large areas were covered by impenetrable forest. We know from finds from Trafalgar Square that elephants and hippopotamus roamed the London area, but we have no signs of human activity.

Between 100,000 and 50,000 years ago temperatures cooled again, and Neanderthals were occupying Europe. Flint axes found in Hillingdon testifiy to Neanderthal presence, but finds are sparse, probably indicating that southern Britain was an inhospitable outpost at this time. Mammoth, ④ woolly rhinoceros, wild horse, reindeer and giant deer roamed a tundra environment.

On the continent modern humans, *Homo sapiens sapiens,* replaced Neanderthals by

Above left Hunting a mammoth; **Above** Palaeolithic flint tools manufactured about 26,000 years ago, found during excavations at Heathrow Airport; **Left** Decorated pottery bowl of about 3300 BC, found at Heathrow. Pottery had been manufactured from around 4500 BC

Above Reconstruction of the valley of the River Colne around 10,000 years ago, in the area of present-day Uxbridge; **Left** This sequence of refitted blades and flakes of flints came from a site in Uxbridge, where tools were made

around 40,000 years ago, but we have no evidence for them in Britain until around 28,000 years ago. In the London area, a small number of flints from this period suggest the presence of hunters following herds on their seasonal migrations.

As the climate began to warm up again after the end of the last Ice Age and the sea level slowly rose, the steppe-tundra environment changed to a landscape of birch and pine. There is more definite evidence now for colonisation of Britain by groups of people who simply walked across the land bridge from the continent before this was flooded once more. These people hunted reindeer and wild horse, and fishing

along the Thames would also have provided an important source of food. The London region would have been largely deserted on a seasonal basis, as mobile groups set up temporary encampments and then moved on to exploit the resources in a fresh area. One such camp was discovered in Uxbridge, west London, on the banks of the River Colne. Thousands of flint tools were found, along with bones showing marks left by butchering.

By around 7000 BC, the London area was covered with a dense forest, which supported a different range of animals, and humans had to adapt their hunting techniques accordingly. The dog was

domesticated and could be used for tracking prey, and the bow and arrow were adopted, allowing animals to be killed at a distance. People may have been able to settle in areas more permanently now, and the gravel islands in the Thames would have been ideal places to camp while fishing.

Estimates of the population are extremely hard to work out for such early times, but between the demise of the Neanderthals (c. 30,000 BC) and the onset of the last glacial period (c. 16,000 BC), the number of people in the London region could probably have fitted comfortably on to just one of London's famous red double-decker buses.

Archaeological fieldwork is the main way in which information about the prehistoric period is learned. **Far left** Taking thin vertical sections of soil samples for geological analysis; **Middle left** Analysis in the laboratory can discover minute evidence of plant and animal remains to reveal evidence of past environments; **Left** This diatom valve (unicellular alga) has been magnified about 5000 times; its presence indicates salinity of water and can therefore give clues as to whether sites would have been occupied in the past; **Left below** Seed cases of the bur-marigold recovered from the pre-Roman Walbrook indicate that it was clean and fast-flowing

Above Reconstruction of a Late Bronze Age fortified settlement, dating to around 1000 BC, in Carshalton, overlooking the valley of the River Wandle which drains into the Thames; **Above right** A Neolithic/Bronze Age blade knife from east London

Neolithic to the Iron Age

The introduction of farming in the Neolithic brought important changes to the landscape of London. Nomadic hunter gatherers were replaced by more settled communities, and widespread clearance of trees for agriculture transformed the appearance of the countryside.

Left An Early Bronze Age barbed and tanged arrowhead from Wimbledon; **Below** Flint, bone and copper knives *c.* 2200–1500 BC, from the Thames in west London, shown together with a modern reconstruction (on the left of the group). The flint and bone examples emulate the form of a copper knife – a symbol of wealth – in commoner materials; **Right** This iron dagger has a sheath made of bronze bands, with a wooden lining. It was found in the Thames at Mortlake, and is dated to 550–450 BC

After nearly half a million years of hunting animals and gathering wild plants, people started deliberately to plant and cultivate crops, domesticate animals and live in permanent settlements. The climate had become much warmer by about 4000 BC, and within a few hundred years humans had cleared large areas for fields, radically changing the landscape. Initially, the local communities practised a simple pastoral agriculture, supplemented by fishing, hunting game and exploiting local wild resources, including fruits and berries. More complex mixed agriculture developed later.

Very little evidence of the habitation sites of these early communities survives, although their earth monuments seem to be located mostly on the gravel terraces on the west side of London, away from the river. After 2000 BC the landscape in this area became increasingly organised, with people now practising a mixed farming regime. The communities lived in small open settlements, with the nearby lands parcelled

3 A criss-cross pattern of ard marks in Southwark dating from the late Neolithic and Early Bronze Age (3000–2000 BC), preserved beneath flood silts

4

Above A near complete Middle Bronze Age jar, found in a ditch of a Late Bronze Age field system. The holes around the rim could have held a skin cover in place, suggesting that the pot was used as a drum; **Left** The jar during reconstruction by conservators

up into fields for agriculture, accessed by droveways. Beyond, the landscape remained pristine, still largely covered in dense woods. 2

At around the same time, or perhaps slightly earlier, communities seem increasingly to have begun to move closer to the Thames, sometimes occupying small islands beside the river. The site where Westminster Abbey and Palace now stand was an island once known as Thorney Island. Pottery of the later Neolithic and Early Bronze Age, as well as flint tools such as arrowheads, scrapers and axes, have been recovered, suggesting that a group of people lived there. Pollen evidence indicates that the area was being farmed, and the inhabitants perhaps revetted the banks of the small streams.

Similar artefacts, though in much greater quantity, have come from once low-lying lands to the south of the Thames beneath modern Southwark. Marks left by ards – a simple tool for ploughing – 3 demonstrate

that the land was being farmed, and cereal pollen recovered from environmental samples adds to this picture of early agriculture. 4 There is even evidence that fields were manured.

Constantly changing river levels must have affected the areas available for habitation and the lives of the people who farmed there. The Thames provided both a healthy food supply and a convenient transport link to other parts of the region (although no boats of this age have so far been found). But to be sited too close to the river could bring disaster if the water level rose rapidly. Communities maintained contact with each other by tracks laid across the areas of marshy ground that increased in the middle of the second millennium BC. 5

Evidence for the later periods is sparse, although there was certainly a thriving resident population when the Romans arrived, bringing with them dramatic changes to the lives of the inhabitants and the landscape of London.

The function of this Bronze Age timber platform on the Isle of Dogs is something of a mystery: relatively few artefacts were associated with it, suggesting that it was probably not a habitation platform, as such sites usually produce much more domestic waste. It may have been used to allow people access into the marsh lands of the area to exploit local resources, such as fish, timber and wildfowl

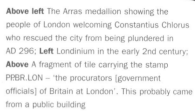

Roman urbanisation

London as a city was a Roman invention – a settlement imposed on the landscape – and its development had a major environmental and cultural impact. Londinium became a meeting point for Briton and Roman, and archaeologists have found many of the public buildings and amenities required for a Roman city.

Some of the coins from a mid-4th-century hoard found in Croydon

Above A 2nd- or 3rd-century copper-alloy incense container associated with the worship of Bacchus; the features and hairstyle appear to depict an Ethiopian. The object provides interesting evidence for the ethnic and religious diversity brought about by the Roman occupation

Right Reconstructed painted wall plaster from a prominent Roman riverfront building on the site of Winchester Palace in Southwark. The painting is shaped to fit into the curved ceiling of a bath-house, and depicts columns decorated with garlands and a figure of Cupid in the centre; it had collapsed face downwards over the hypocaust; **Bottom right** Part of a typical late Roman mosaic floor from a building on Bishopsgate

Left Elaborately decorated pottery was among the many high-quality goods imported to Roman London. This example from the amphitheatre depicts gladiators fighting bulls

Newgate, one of the six gates controlling access to the city

Founded by AD 47, only four years after the invasion of Britain by the Emperor Claudius, London was established at the lowest point on the Thames where it could be bridged and where a port could be sited. The great advantage of the Thames is that it forms a natural navigable route from the North Sea into central England. ①

London's early status is unclear: it perhaps began as a community of traders, or it may have had an administrative or military origin. ② The Roman historian Tacitus provides us with the earliest historical record of London. He describes it on the eve of the revolt by Boudica, Queen of the Iceni, as 'not distinguished by the title of colony yet exceedingly famous for its wealth of traders and commercial traffic'. With its timber buildings ③ and muddy streets, first-century London must have had the appearance and character of a frontier town. Certain elements were surveyed and planned from the outset, however, such as the road system from the south across the bridge and the grid of streets around the site of the later forum.

The exact size of the town's population is uncertain, but may have been as much as 10,000 by AD 60 and perhaps more than double that at its peak in the early second century. The houses, shops and other properties were closely spaced, and the variety of building types reflected the ethnic diversity of the settlement. ④ This first timber town was destroyed in the Boudican revolt of AD 60, but London was soon re-established, defended by ditches and greatly expanded. The 70s and 80s saw a massive investment in a programme of public building, with the construction of the forum-basilica, amphitheatre, public baths and other infrastructure – all important symbols of Romanisation.

The later Roman town differed substantially from the boomtown of the first century and it suffered a serious setback when it was destroyed by fire in about AD 125. London now declined in importance, and while new timber buildings appeared on many properties, there were also more open spaces. However, although less busy than in earlier centuries, late Roman London remained an important town both economically and politically. A fort was constructed and stone houses were built, with wealthy citizens maintaining both town houses in London ⑤ and villas in the countryside.

Beyond the Roman city lay an agricultural hinterland, which provided produce for the large urban population. Archaeologists have found little evidence of suburban growth around the city, suggesting that there was adequate space within the walled city for the population. ⑥ On the south bank of the river, a major settlement in Southwark formed around the bridgehead, stretching back along the main Roman road approaching from the south. This had quite a different character from the city on the north side of the bridge. Smaller communities lived in villages such as those found on the banks of the River Lea at Bow and in north London in Enfield. Rural villas are a rare phenomenon in the Greater London area – they tended to be sited further from the Roman city, particularly in Kent, although one has been partially excavated at Beddington near Croydon.

Above After abandonment by the Romans, the old city would have fallen into ruin; **Left** Mysterious 'dark earth' is clearly visible as a layer over 1 metre thick lying over the abandoned remains of the Roman amphitheatre, giving little clue as to what went on here before London was reoccupied in the 9th century; **Above right** Loomweights, indicative of cloth production, found in a Saxon building on the Royal Opera House site; **Right** The jaw bone of a pig used as a trial piece for carving with complicated designs of Scandinavian style

Saxon towns & villages

Archaeologists find this period one of the most puzzling, as there is so little evidence for activity found in the London region.

A silver penny of King Alfred, minted in London *c.* 880, with a stylised portrait of Alfred and a monogram of the letters LVNDONIA for 'London'

By the late fourth century Rome found it increasingly difficult to defend the frontiers of its empire and Britain was at risk from attack both from within and from the continent. The collapse of Roman rule and withdrawal of troops from Britain in the early fifth century left London at the mercy of barbarian attack, and the political and economic basis for urban life quickly dissolved. These barbarian tribes included the Angles, Saxons, Jutes and Frisians. The city, like many throughout England, seems to have been abandoned, **1** and sixth- and early seventh-century settlements may have been dispersed and small. Often all that remains of the houses and yards of the inhabitants is a layer of mixed soil, known to archaeologists as 'dark earth'. **2**

The main settlement of 'London' was re-established as 'Lundenwic', outside the Roman walls in the area where Covent Garden now lies. Traces of it remain in street names such as 'Strand' meaning 'beach', and 'Aldwych' meaning 'old town'. Lundenwic first developed during the seventh century and was a flourishing trading settlement by the eighth century when it is mentioned by the early historian Bede. Its limits may have been formed by the old Roman road of Holborn and Oxford Street on the north, and a line roughly to the north of Trafalgar Square to the west. The eastern side may have stretched as far as the River Fleet or perhaps stopped near Kingsway.

A pattern of small streets and alleys has been traced within Lundenwic, which were

Above left Postholes within a shallow depression – all that remains of a Saxon house in Hammersmith; **Left** The old Roman amphitheatre would still have been discernible in the Saxon landscape of the 11th century, but with the arena as little more than a depression in the ground now covered by a street lined with wattle and timber houses. A timber hall on the old north bank was perhaps the forerunner of today's Guildhall; **Below** A late Saxon comb made of bone and carved and decorated antler

lined with small timber houses and shops. All manner of trades and light industries were practised, such as weaving, ③ boneworking ④ and metalworking, and archaeology has revealed that houses, shops and small shacks for carrying out industries were all concentrated on a single plot.

Much of the rest of the London region was rural land, dotted with farmsteads whose occupants cultivated the nearby fields. ⑤ One such farmstead was found by archaeologists in the 1960s, just to the south of Lundenwic, beneath Downing Street. Floors and the lower part of the timber walls of the house were still intact, and a farm enclosure surrounded it. London's cathedral at this time was St Paul's, still sited inside the old Roman city.

There may also have been a large church to the south of Lundenwic on Thorney Island, where Westminster Abbey now stands.

By the middle of the ninth century the Vikings were beginning their raids on England. Lundenwic was a particular target and they were able to sail up the Thames and set fire to the city. In response to this threat Londoners moved back inside the old walled Roman city – although it must have been partly ruinous by then it would still have afforded them some protection. ⑥ This new settlement was supported by King Alfred and was called Lundenburg – '-burg' being added to the name given to new towns founded by King Alfred. Based partly on the old Roman town, new streets were also created which altered its character

and resulted in the current layout of the city – a hybrid of the old Roman foundation and the later Saxon and medieval town. ⑦ The settlement was originally centred around Aethelred's Hythe (or dock), but excavations show that the town soon expanded up the hill away from the river as the population grew and more goods were brought there to trade.

On the south bank of the river was the South Work (or defence), now known as Southwark, a settlement based on the defences built around the bridgehead. It was attacked by the Vikings on numerous occasions.

2 **Above left** An early woodcut showing a densely occupied London surrounded by open spaces; **Above** Braun & Hogenburg's map of London, 1572. Fields still adjoin the old City wall in places, with houses lining the thoroughfares leading from the city

London becomes a World City

Over the last 2000 years London has grown from an outpost of the Roman Empire into one of the world's greatest cities.

Below The remains of a medieval manor in Walthamstow, once owned by Warwick the Kingmaker (who helped depose Henry VI and bring Edward IV to the throne in 1460), would once have stood in isolated grandeur; now evidence of countryside is only barely discernible in the distance beyond a sea of late 19th- and 20th-century housing

Above 19th-century commentators were well aware of the effects of the housing boom on London's rural hinterland, as this cartoon by George Cruikshank, entitled 'London going out of town or the march of bricks and mortar', makes clear; **Right** *From Pentonville Road looking west: Evening, 1884* by John O'Connor (detail) illustrates the new ease of movement of people both in and out of and around London, with St Pancras Station and the Midland Railway Hotel, and, in the foreground, horse-drawn trams

Far left The Great Drain of St Mary Spital; Left Houses in Uxbridge High Street from a painting of c. 1800; Above 18th-century houses in Spitalfields

At the time of the Norman Conquest in 1066, London was bordered by Southwark, Westminster and a number of outlying villages, but the population of the region was quite small. ① By 1500 London had expanded considerably to accommodate the number of inhabitants, which had grown to perhaps as many as 100,000. ②

Initially the area enclosed within the City walls was not fully occupied, and archaeologists have discovered that much of the eastern part was uninhabited until around 1150. In the following years London began to expand along the major roads leading out of the City. Monasteries were founded in open land alongside these thoroughfares, such as St John's and St Mary's in Clerkenwell, St Bartholomew's in Smithfield and St Mary Spital on Bishopsgate. ③ The routes between the City and these monasteries then soon became lined with houses. Behind were open fields where the inhabitants could grow food and the area was also used for light industry.

Fleet Street and the Strand linked London's commercial centre with the political, religious and royal centre at Westminster, and this area was soon filled with the fine mansions of aristocrats and bishops who wanted to be close to both centres. The suburb of Southwark also expanded along its main highway south (now Borough High

Street). Although this area seems to have been poorer than the north side of the river, it was chosen as the site of the townhouses of several nobles and church dignitaries including the Bishops of Winchester.

The outlying settlements were not originally part of London. Some were little more than small villages while others, such as Kingston and Uxbridge, were important towns in their own right. Archaeologists have uncovered substantial parts of both of these thriving market towns. ④

From the seventeenth century to the present day, London has grown to such an extent that many of these outlying villages have now been absorbed as suburbs of a vast metropolis covering 325 square kilometres. By looking at old maps it is possible to trace the spread of early modern London, and archaeology helps to fill in the details. Often we know that there were houses in a particular area, but it is only by excavating them that we can understand the lifestyles of people who lived in them. For instance hundreds of new houses were built in Spitalfields between 1660 and 1740, ⑤ and excavation of many of these has given us new insights into the status and living conditions of their inhabitants.

The expansion of London in the nineteenth century was the most dramatic and had the

most far-reaching consequences. ⑥ The cause was the rapid growth in population, but its enormous spread was facilitated by the invention and expansion of the railways. Before the railways it would have taken hours for someone to travel from Enfield to the City. Now, new houses could be built at much greater distances from London as workers could travel into the centre to work in a relatively short period of time. Initially the housing was built around the stations, but soon whole districts were created and the old rural landscape was changed forever. ⑦ By the 1940s, London's population had soared to 8,000,000.

This elaborate Westerwald jug with 'peacock eye' decoration was imported from the Rhineland in the 17th century

London's rivers

Above Bronze Age side-looped spearhead from the foreshore at Vauxhall; **Right** Archaeologists taking cores from the foreshore in order to map buried sediments and test for environmental evidence of earlier landscapes

The Thames

The Thames provides an important route for trade and communication to London; it also forms a barrier between its north and south banks.

Above The lead head of a 14th-century stick puppet, found on the foreshore; **Below** Recording a Victorian barge bed on the City foreshore

Left Kingston Bridge from the east, showing the proximity of the medieval revetment to the present river; **Above** The Thames as commercial highway with newly built warehouses lining the north bank, shown in Thomas Miles Richardson's painting *The City from Bankside, 1820s*

A medieval mill operated by tidal flow near Tower Bridge, with elm floor planks well preserved in waterlogged deposits

Left The skeletal remains of some of the 76 horse burials found in Westminster. Analysis shows that most of the horses were stocky adult males, and the location of the burial ground on a street still called Horseferry Road suggests that some at least of the horses would have pulled the ferries; **Above** An ornate medieval copper alloy horse harness pendant found on the Southwark foreshore

The River Thames is the main reason why London is sited where it is. It was a major route for goods and people until the decline of London's docks in the 1960s. But before the end of the last Ice Age, Britain was still joined to the continent and the Thames was probably a tributary of the River Rhine. Like all rivers, the Thames deposited silt in some areas and eroded its banks in others, and over thousands of years its course has altered dramatically. It was once much wider and shallower than it is today – over 450 m wide in AD 100 ➊ whereas now it is only 200 m wide. Lack of available land for building has meant that over the centuries people have built out into it, making the river narrower. As a result of forcing the same amount of water through a smaller space, the river flows faster and cuts a deeper channel.

In general, sea level has been rising over the last 10,000 years, forcing the tidal head (the point at which the river stops being tidal) further and further upstream. At times, however, sea level falls and the tidal head moves downstream. In 2000 BC it lay above Westminster; in AD 100 it was at London Bridge. By AD 1200 it was above Westminster again and it is now at Teddington. Any changes in the level of the river must have had an effect on the lives of people in the past. When sea level fell, boats which could once have been brought in on the tide would not have been able to reach the port, leading to the decline of trade and the loss of livelihoods. When the river rose, whole settlements might be flooded, destroying homes and land.

Roman London was sited on a terrace which levelled out to a beach on the river at a point where the tide could still take boats. ➋ The south side of the river was made up of a series of low-lying islands which were regularly flooded. The main settlement of Southwark was sited on the largest and highest of these islands, opposite Londinium.

Roads in the past were often hazardous and traffic slow, so the Thames was a favoured route for people as well as trade. Wherrymen rowed passengers from jetties up, down and across the river. The royal palace at Westminster had two jetties, so that the king and his courtiers could be transported quickly and conveniently. One was discovered when the Clock Tower for the Houses of Parliament was built. Long journeys would be timed to coincide with the tide – otherwise the journey could take much longer. In the future, the Thames may once again have an important role to play in solving London's transport problems.

As it flows to the sea the river naturally deposits sediment, which builds up and tends to impede navigation. Dredging is regularly carried out to remove this sediment, bringing up with the mud large amounts of finds. Many important artefacts were brought to light during these operations in the nineteenth century, and more were discovered when new bridges were built over the river. Some of London's most spectacular objects have been found in this way, from the famous Battersea Shield to Saxon swords, prehistoric flints and objects from the Roman and medieval periods. ➌

Study of geological samples and plant remains has shown that the Walbrook stream looked like this before the Romans arrived in AD 43

London's other rivers

Many other rivers once flowed into the Thames in the London region but only a few can now be seen.

By far the largest of London's other rivers was the Lea, which formed the old boundary between Middlesex and Essex. The Lea was once navigable and was used by the Danes when they attacked the south-east of England in the ninth century. King Alfred is said to have sailed up this river after these raiders in AD 896. By the fifteenth century it was becoming blocked and a new cut was constructed; very early locks were also built to aid navigation. Industry was attracted to the Lea, as well as other rivers, because their flow supplied power; mills were once a common feature, now remembered for instance in the name Temple Mills in Leyton. ❶

The Wandle, in south London, flows from Carshalton northwards through Morden to Wandsworth where it joins the Thames. Canalisation means that it is now a fairly small river but it was once much larger. Archaeologists have found numerous settlements built alongside it, as well as an important monastery at Merton. Light industry, such as William Morris' factory in Merton, was also drawn to it in the nineteenth century because of its fast-flowing, unpolluted waters. ❷

❷ **Above** Detail of one of the stained glass windows at St Mary the Virgin, Merton, made by Morris & Co from designs by Edward Burne-Jones; **Below** Oak paint brushes dating to the 18th century found during excavations at the site of William Morris's factory on the River Wandle

Right Cleaning the brick walls of the gear pit at the early 19th-century Bennett's Mill, found on the River Wandle at Merton; **Far right** Watercolour of Jacob's Island in 1887, by J. Stewart, showing the mill stream which ran into the Thames near the Design Museum on the south bank. Charles Dickens mentions this place in *Oliver Twist* as '... surrounded by a muddy ditch, six or eight feet deep and fifteen or twenty feet wide when the tide is in, once called Mill Pond', and excavations have found the former stream filled with 17th- to 19th-century domestic rubbish from the overhanging houses

Buildings gradually encroached on the smaller rivers until they were canalised – like the Fleet, shown here on an engraved woodcut map of *c.* 1588 – and finally built right over

Above left Badge worn by a retainer of the Talbot family, found during excavations in the Fleet valley; **Above** The physical presence of the valley of the Fleet is still evident in the view today looking north (up the old river valley) towards Holborn Viaduct from Farringdon Road

Although they are now either hidden or have long since dried up, many other important rivers once flowed through the city. Of these the Fleet was the largest and most famous. Its source lay in Hampstead Heath, and from here it ran past today's Kings Cross and down the line of modern Farringdon Road, where it is now carried beneath the street in a sewer. It formed the edge of the Roman and medieval cities and was crossed by five bridges. At its mouth, perhaps 150 m wide during the Roman period, the Fleet was navigable. Over time the river was canalised and became known as the 'Fleet Ditch', ❸ a notoriously foul-smelling open sewer until the nineteenth century. The old river valley is still visible in the slope from Smithfield Market and Holborn. ❹

The Walbrook was a smaller river than the Fleet and ran through the heart of the City. Its course took it past the site of the Bank of England, and down to the Thames. It provided a distinct break in the topography of Roman London and there was a marked change in the character of the settlement on either side. During the Roman period it seems to have been a favoured place for

ritually discarding artefacts, particularly metalwork and human skulls, ❺ which have been recovered by antiquarians and archaeologists during various building works. The stream was revetted with planks to prevent the sides slipping in and was probably only about 4 m wide in Roman times. By the medieval period the passage of the stream through the city wall had become blocked, causing it to back up and a marsh to form in the Moorfields area.

Another of London's famous old rivers was the Tyburn. This also rose in Hampstead and flowed down through Green Park to where Buckingham Palace now stands. At this point the river spread out into a wide valley, stretching from present-day Downing Street around to Buckingham Palace Road where it met the River Westbourne. Archaeologists can map old river deltas by studying the records of boreholes, excavations and building works to create contour plans of the river valleys and the islands which they surrounded. Within the Tyburn delta the largest and most famous island was Thorney, where the royal Palace and Abbey of Westminster were sited. ❻

Above The prehistoric river course of the Tyburn at its junction with the Thames, superimposed on the modern landscape of Westminster, gives a clear impression of the area of Thorney Island; **Below** Surveying the medieval and later revetments of tidal Deptford Creek near its confluence with the Thames

Above middle Archaeologists recording the massive oak timbers of the riverside face of the mid-1st-century quay, with bracing timbers on the landward side (centre) and the threshold for contemporary warehousing (background); **Above** Reconstruction showing the construction methods used by the Romans

Land reclamation

Since the Roman period, Londoners have gradually gained about 100 metres of land from the river on the north bank of the Thames.

The investigation of London's river defences has long been one of the central aspects of the city's archaeology, though digging these sites is often difficult and dangerous. Ancient timber river walls can be as much as 7 m below modern ground level, and often the sites are subject to flooding. Since the Roman period, Londoners have reclaimed land, continually encroaching into the river for a distance of about 100 m.

This process began in a small way in AD 52 (as revealed by tree-ring dating), **1** while the first major port facility was constructed in AD 63–64. It was possibly an imperial project carried out by the army to restore the town's infrastructure after its destruction during the Boudican revolt of AD 60. A massive quay was built, consisting of stacks of horizontally laid squared oak baulks, now beautifully preserved by waterlogging. **2**

Top left Model showing Roman land reclamation beside the bridge across the Thames; **Left** The eastern end of the Roman riverside wall, discovered beneath the brick inner curtain wall of the Tower of London, is still visible today

The success of London's port is best illustrated by the successive piecemeal reclamation of the foreshore during the second century AD. In around AD 200–25 an attempt was made to restore a unified river frontage by constructing a new timber quay with associated buildings similar to those of the earlier periods but further out into the river. **3** By AD 250–70 the port was in serious decline, and soon afterwards a stone defensive riverside wall was built, severing London from its river and preventing any further revival of the port. **4**

With the resettlement of the abandoned Roman city by King Alfred in the late ninth century, reclamation of land from the Thames continued. **5** At Queenhithe the king established a dock, initially a 'beach market' where trade was conducted directly from vessels on the Thames foreshore. A second dock was later created at Billingsgate and these two points provided the focus for rapid development of the city's waterfront.

From the beginning of the twelfth century the character of the waterfront changed dramatically. Up to this time reclamation was fairly small in scale, and the use of private

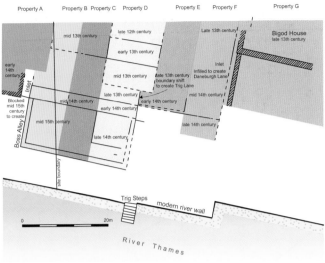

Far left top Recording a section of the timber-laced embankment dating to 1045 forming the eastern side of Queenhithe; **Far left** This stave revetment was built in 1121; **Left** Plan showing how individual properties gradually expanded their river frontages, altering the face of the medieval City waterfront

wharves as well as public docks meant that waterfront space was at a premium. Now property owners desperately needed to expand – and the only available direction was out into the river. ⑥ Numerous excavations have revealed that substantial timber river walls were constructed in a variety of styles, ⑦ consolidated with massive dumps of material, often waste from other parts of London. This material provides archaeologists with some of the finest groups of finds from London and, since they are associated with timbers which can dated precisely by tree-ring dating, they have helped to establish chronologies for the recovered pottery and other artefacts.

Reclamation provided a flat waterside platform on which trade and industry could be carried out, a river wall against which vessels could dock, and the opportunity to extend any buildings on a property southwards. The lifespan of the wooden river walls was generally only about 20–25 years before they needed replacement. Rather than rebuild the existing structure, it was more cost-effective simply to expand yet further into the river. As a result, up to 40 m of land was artificially gained from the

river at some sites during the twelfth century alone. Up to the thirteenth century stone riverside walls tended to be confined to properties belonging to the Crown or wealthy religious institutions, but as prosperity increased they were also built on commercial properties, especially in the City. Stone construction helped extend the life of each advance, and by the end of the fifteenth century the rate of reclamation had considerably slowed. Much of the present-day line of the waterfront was established by the seventeenth century.

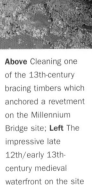

Above Cleaning one of the 13th-century bracing timbers which anchored a revetment on the Millennium Bridge site; **Left** The impressive late 12th/early 13th-century medieval waterfront on the site of the old Billingsgate Fish Market

Above left The late 1st-century quay, cutting into the pier base of the first of London's bridges;
Right Tree-ring dating of the timber piles beneath medieval London bridge has helped to provide the construction date of the end of the 12th century

Bridges

People have been constructing bridges over the Thames for almost 2000 years. The first was built by the Romans from the City to Southwark and the most recent, the Millennium Bridge, also crosses the Thames from the City to Southwark.

Excavations at Kingston in 1985 exposed the remains of the original 13th-century stone and timber bridge just downstream from its modern counterpart

Today, the Thames in London is crossed by many different bridges, but for centuries there was only one fixed crossing over the river that had to be constantly rebuilt. London's first bridge was constructed by the Romans, ❶ probably just downstream from where the current London Bridge now stands. When the Romans invaded Britain in AD 43 they would have forded the Thames, but eventually the need for a bridge became overwhelming. Probably built by the end of the first century AD, it crossed the river at its narrowest point, from the high ground in the City to the main island in Southwark. ❷ At that time Southwark consisted of numerous islands, all of which would have been linked by small bridges.

The Roman bridge had a series of stone piers and a timber superstructure. It may have had a drawbridge, as much of the

Roman harbour lay upstream and the bridge may not have been high enough to allow boats to sail beneath. Massive oak timbers uncovered in Pudding Lane perhaps represent the beginning of the bridge on the northern side. The ultimate fate of this Roman bridge is uncertain, but it is possible that it was either swept away by the river or simply fell into decay.

A series of timber bridge abutments and caissons, the earliest of which date back to *c.* 987–1032, provide evidence for the medieval bridge over the Thames. Most of the successive timber bridges were washed away by floods, which left behind thick layers of mud uncovered by archaeologists in areas that were otherwise dry land.

PETER JACKSON

Above Medieval London bridge, like its predecessor, lay a small distance to the east of today's bridge

Below Found during excavations prior to the building of the Millennium Bridge, this copper alloy strap-end dating to the 13th or 14th century shows a stylised depiction of a tree with the legend JESUS NAZERENUS around the outer edge

Below Stone revetments revealed during the construction of the Millennium Bridge footbridge

The first stone bridge (*c.* 1176–1209) was more durable, but even this partially collapsed on two occasions, immortalised in the well-known children's rhyme: once in 1281–82 when five arches fell down, and again in January 1437 when two more collapsed at its southern end. A massive rebuilding and repair programme lasted for the next forty years, with the bridge's stone arches supported by timber piles rammed deep into the river mud. ③ This London Bridge, famous for the buildings and shops which lined the street that ran across it, ④ was replaced in 1831 by a new bridge designed by John Rennie. This bridge was in turn replaced in 1967–71 and transported to Arizona.

In the medieval period, the next bridge over the Thames was at Kingston, built a little before 1200. The abutment and four piers of this stone bridge have been found on the east side of the river, just beyond where the current bridge now stands. Later alterations joined the two piers nearest the land to create a causeway on to the bridge. By the seventeenth century the piers no longer stood in the water, showing just how much of the river had been reclaimed.

The Thames was not bridged again in central London until a crossing was built at Westminster in around 1750. Not surprisingly there was great opposition from the ferrymen to another bridge as it posed a threat to the living they made from carrying people from one side of the river to the other. Hungerford Bridge, Tower Bridge and a succession of others finally created the modern appearance of the Thames – very different from most of its history. Many of these bridges have also been rebuilt, affording archaeologists opportunities for excavation. ⑤ The first new bridge for some time, the Millennium Bridge, was opened to the public in 2002. It brings the story of London's bridges full circle, as it crosses the Thames from the City to Southwark, along the same route as London's first bridge.

Right *Blackfriars Bridge, 1798* by Nathaniel Black and Thomas Rowlandson. The bottlenecks caused by the hectic human and animal traffic over London's bridges was to lead to the rule of 'left-hand' traffic still in use on our roads today

1st-century Roman brooch depicting three men in a boat, with the prow in the form of a bird

Boats

Evidence for ancient boats turns up in two main ways: either actual examples of craft are found preserved in rivers or creeks, or fragments of boats are found reused in other wooden structures such as riverside timber walls. One of the most fascinating discoveries was made on a site in Southwark, between London Bridge and Tower Bridge. Archaeologists excavating a group of Tudor fishponds next to the river unexpectedly came across a large part of the side of a boat reused to edge one of the ponds. ❶ The boat was a thirteenth- or early fourteenth-century galley. Three oar ports and cut-outs for the benches where the oarsmen sat were still visible, and even its gunwale survived. Other fragments of boats recovered in this way include part of an early Frisian boat and timbers from a

'cog' ❷ – a type of ship used by the merchants of Hansa in the Baltic – found reused in a cesspit at Westminster.

The first partially complete Roman boat to come to light was found opposite Westminster in 1910, deep within the foundations of a new building for the London County Council. It caused quite a stir at the time and was paraded through the city to the London Museum. Probably originally about 20 m long and 5 m wide, it had a rounded bottom, suggesting that it was a small merchant ship of perhaps about 60 tonnes. It probably sank in around AD 300. Two other Roman boats have also been found, both flat-bottomed barges, presumably for transferring goods from larger ships to the port and up and down

Excavating the shipbreaker's yard at Rotherhithe where *HMS Temeraire* (the 'Fighting Temeraire' of J. M. W. Turner's painting) was broken up in 1838. Much of the massive bracing behind the dock was, unsurprisingly, constructed from old ships' timbers

Right 17th-century ships' timbers at Bellamy's Wharf reused as land ties for a dock inlet and river wall. The large curved white-lead painted timber is a virtually complete stem (the main upright timber at the bow of the ship); **Below** The Golden Hind at St Saviour's dock today

the smaller rivers which fed into the Thames. One, dating to the fourth century, was found abandoned in a creek beneath what is now Guy's Hospital in Southwark, and the other was found in 1962 near the mouth of the River Fleet. **3** This one was built in the second century AD and sank while carrying a cargo of building stone, probably for the construction of the city wall.

We also have examples of later boats, and not just from the Thames. An important group was found in the Thames in 1970 when a new road was built at Blackfriars. Among the Blackfriars boats were two from the medieval period and one dating from the seventeenth century, preserved in the old river silts. Excavation was hazardous as archaeologists had to work in deep coffer dams built to keep the river out. The more

complete medieval boat **4** was built of oak, probably between 1380 and 1415, and sank between 1480 and 1500. It measured about 14.6 m long and 4.3 m wide and was thought to have been able to carry about 7.5 tonnes. It probably had a mast carrying a square sail which could be removed whenever the boat passed beneath low bridges. The ship was designed to sail along the Thames and its tributaries carrying a cargo of wheat, tiles and other commodities. A second boat nearby was a 'lighter' – a smaller boat for carrying goods from vessels anchored in mid-stream – and at the time it sank was carrying a cargo of stone. The proximity of the two boats suggests that they sank as a result of a disastrous collision. An early medieval log boat, **5** little more than a rowing boat, was found on the western bank of the River Lea.

Top The Clapton logboat, dated to AD 950–1000, was made from an entire oak log. In hollowing out the inside, a transverse bulkhead was left to stiffen the boat and provide a seat; **Above** A reconstruction of the logboat proved its suitability as a craft designed to carry cargo through the slack waters of Hackney marshes; **Below** A Saxon paddle from Southwark

Left Reconstruction of a section across a Roman ship in progress at the Museum of London; **Far left** A conservator cleans the elaborately carved top of a 'bitt' (a vertical timber on the deck through which the rigging ropes pass) from a large 17th-century ship found at Bellamy's Wharf, Southwark

Infrastructure

Top left This trackway at Bramcote Grove was laid across marsh about 3500 years ago to provide access from high ground in the south to Bermondsey island in the north; **Above** Bronze Age timber platform at Atlas Wharf in east London; **Left** One of the stakes used to secure the platform at Atlas Wharf

Thoroughfares

Although the Thames has been London's main thoroughfare for most of its history, roads and paths have always been important means of access across London.

Some of our earliest evidence for tracks comes from the Bronze Age. Changing river levels at this period often made land accessible only at certain times of the year, and even then across boggy ground, so wooden tracks were laid across the marshland. **1** Where the ground has remained waterlogged, archaeologists can still find such tracks, nearly 4000 years later. Some joined one settlement to another, while others provided access to the river's edge where people could hunt and fish. They range from complex lattices of hurdles to simple lines of oak logs. **2**

More familiar are the roads laid on dry ground between settlements and within towns. The Romans are, to many people, synonymous with roads, and the road network certainly played an important role in the Romanisation of Britain. The major Roman routes around the island are well known and often lie beneath present-day thoroughfares, but in London much of the street pattern changed from the ninth century onwards, so Roman roads here are found beneath modern buildings.

Below This early 17th-century cobbled road just north of the Thames survived to its full width and was buried, along with the remains of the adjacent property to the west, under a thick deposit of debris from the Great Fire of 1666; **Right** The cobbled surface of medieval St Pancras Lane under excavation at 1 Poultry

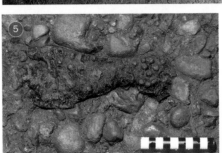

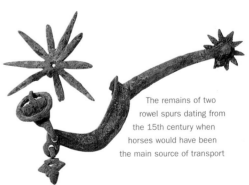

Far left View along the line of the gravel surface of a Roman road, leading south from the Cripplegate fort to the settlement's main east–west road; **Above left** A side street off the main road in Southwark with the wheel ruts made by carts clearly visible; **Left** The remains of a Roman shoe on a cobbled road; **Above** Drains often flanked Roman roads; this box-drain made from oak planks was found at 1 Poultry in the City

Above The pattern of London's Roman streets was first mapped by Stukeley in 1724

In both the Roman and medieval periods, most roads in London were made of gravel rammed down to create a compact surface. ③ Gravel is the underlying subsoil across much of the London region and was therefore in plentiful supply. Occasional evidence of the traffic that used the roads survives in the form of cartwheel tracks ④ or even the imprint of a shoe. ⑤

The main east–west road in the Roman city ran from the forum (beneath modern Leadenhall market) through the walls at Newgate before continuing on to Silchester; it is thought that it formed one of the earliest elements in the laying out of London. The road was about 9 m wide and was in use until at least the later fourth century, by which time the surface had been re-laid twelve times – the result of the wear and tear of thousands of pedestrians and carts – and it rose by 1.2 m in the process. The gravelled surface was cambered to allow rainwater to run off into drains lining the street. ⑥

Other roads, for instance one to St Albans at Brockley and another approaching London Bridge, were of a similar size, while the road to Chichester, called Stane Street, was up to 16 m wide – the size of a modern highway.

Smaller roads, typically 5 m wide, formed side streets. They did not always run at right angles to the main streets, showing that London was not laid out on a rectilinear grid pattern even in the Roman period. ⑦ Large buildings would have lined the main streets, while smaller shops and houses stood along the side streets.

The remains of two rowel spurs dating from the 15th century when horses would have been the main source of transport

Left Later roads, such as this 18th-century street in Bermondsey, were often built from stone cobbles, sometimes granite, mined in south-west England

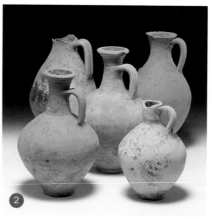

1

Left A 1st-century well, made from reused silver-fir barrels; **Above** A group of 2nd-century flagons thrown down a Roman timber well at Spitalfields just outside the city. Wells often prove rich sources of material for the archaeologist, with objects dropped or ritually placed into them, or simply discarded when the wells went out of use and became convenient rubbish pits

Above Archaeologists cleaning the original cross-braces of the western well at Gresham Street. The 5-metre-deep shaft was constructed in about AD 63; **Below** A reconstruction of the water-lifting mechanism of the eastern well

Water supply

Any settlement requires a plentiful supply of clean water – for drinking, cooking and washing away foul water, and for industry.

Archaeologists have discovered water-holes and ponds dating to the prehistoric period, while the earliest Roman facilities consist of timber-lined wells, dug deep into the gravel. 1 There is a particular concentration on the north side of Queen Victoria Street, suggesting that there was a spring line here. Roman wells often had 'ritual' offerings thrown into them when they went out of use, perhaps to placate the earth deity that had been violated when they had been dug. These deposits include entire ceramic vessels, 2 often with a hole deliberately made in them, and dead animals, especially dogs. On the whole such wells were dug by individuals in their own back yards, although some might have been communal, perhaps sited on vacant land or in the street.

It is not always easy for archaeologists to be certain whether a channel was used to bring water in or to carry it away. One timber-lined feature running along the road approaching the bridge in Southwark could have been either a drain or a small-scale aqueduct. Perhaps the most remarkable examples of a water-supply system found in London are four deep early Roman wells 3 containing fragments of water-lifting mechanisms, probably powered by people working capstans or treadmills. 4 Two of these were found on a site near the fort at Gresham Street, but the devices in each well worked in different ways.

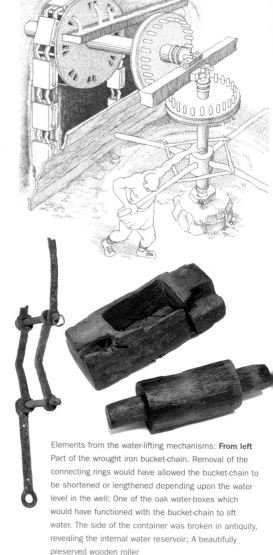

Elements from the water-lifting mechanisms: **From left** Part of the wrought iron bucket-chain. Removal of the connecting rings would have allowed the bucket-chain to be shortened or lengthened depending upon the water level in the well; One of the oak water-boxes which would have functioned with the bucket-chain to lift water. The side of the container was broken in antiquity, revealing the internal water reservoir; A beautifully preserved wooden roller

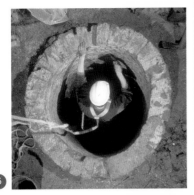

Above Part of a lead pipe associated with the Great Conduit, carrying water 3 km to the City from the River Tyburn; **Right** Wooden water pipes found in Southwark; bored from elm trunks, they were tapered at one end and enlarged at the other so that the pipes could be fitted together. With a lifespan of only about 25 years before the ends split, wooden water pipes were replaced by iron pipes towards the end of the 18th century; **Below right** An early 19th-century water tank lined with 18th-century tin-glazed wall tiles,which may have been used for storing oysters in Giltspur Street

Public well pumps were common in the City until the mid 19th century. **Below left** This pump still stands at Aldgate; **Below right** Detail of the waterspout of the pump at Cornhill

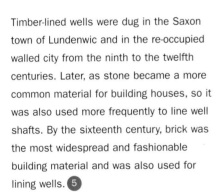

Timber-lined wells were dug in the Saxon town of Lundenwic and in the re-occupied walled city from the ninth to the twelfth centuries. Later, as stone became a more common material for building houses, so it was also used more frequently to line well shafts. By the sixteenth century, brick was the most widespread and fashionable building material and was also used for lining wells. ⑤

More elaborate forms of water supply have also been found, which reflect a collective attitude towards providing water on a much larger scale than the wells for individual houses or small groups of dwellings. Perhaps the largest was the Great Conduit in Cheapside, first built in 1236–45. The rebuilt version, dating to 1286, was found almost intact beneath the street. Stairs from the street led down to a door to an underground chamber ⑥ with a stone-vaulted ceiling. This was a communal supply, free to all, and was fed by pipes which stretched all the way from the River Tyburn in west London.

Monastic communities were famed for the elaborate systems they constructed and in London there is evidence for several types. Many simply had wells, but at the Priory and Hospital of St Mary Spital, water was piped from a well known as Snecockeswell to a large reservoir, ⑦ and then around the precincts. At the nunneries of St Mary Clerkenwell and St Mary's at Holywell, as their names imply, wells were built on the site of springs, which provided a copious supply of water. The three monasteries in Clerkenwell, St Mary's, St John's and the Charterhouse, all had access to a supply from north London which was carried through lead pipes to each monastery. At the Charterhouse the water was piped to a central conduit before being distributed around the monastery, as shown in a remarkable fifteenth-century map.

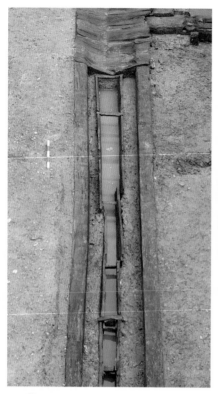

Gold finger ring lost in a Roman cesspit at Gresham Street near the military fort in the city

Drainage & waste disposal

Drains and rubbish pits often provide
a wealth of archaeological information.

1 Carefully constructed Roman box drains, often with complex joints, display the skills of the Roman carpenter. **Above** The central timber drain running under the Roman amphitheatre arena, revealed by removing the original plank roof still visible at the top of the photograph; **Below** A well-preserved rectangular box reused as a drainage sump within the timber amphitheatre of AD 70

Of equal importance to the provision of water is a means of draining it away as well as removing foul waste. The earliest roadside drains in the first century consisted of well-constructed timber boxes, neatly set into trenches along the edges of the roads. **1** By the third century roads were often flanked by rather basic ditches, the sides simply retained by a variety of structures reusing whatever scraps of wood were available. These ditches were often also used as rubbish dumps – no doubt the source unpleasant smells, especially in hot weather.

The most impressive system for water disposal yet found in Roman London is an extraordinarily well-preserved stone and tile culvert, **2** buried deep beneath modern buildings. It originally ran for a distance of

more than 80 m from a stone building down to the River Thames; one 20-m stretch was found complete with a square manhole shaft **3** at its upper end. As the structure was up to 1.8 m in height inside it seems unlikely that it served just one building and may have been connected to several, or even to a bathhouse or the forum.

Provisions for removing waste water did not change much in later periods, with timber, stone or even open drains carrying it away to rivers, though often it was simply dumped in the street, making London a highly insanitary and noxious place at times.

Monastic houses managed the problem in a more sophisticated and better organised way, since such large communities were served. Archaeologists have uncovered the great drain at St Mary Spital which carried waste water beneath the main road, Bishopsgate, down towards the River Walbrook; and an even more impressive structure was discovered at Bermonsdey Priory. ④ The great drain at Westminster Abbey emptied on to the river's foreshore which was washed clean at each high tide. However, as the population grew, dumping waste straight into rivers meant that they became more and more polluted and fewer fish were able to survive in them. The Fleet was notorious as an open sewer, and even the Thames itself eventually became so polluted that Parliament had to abandon Westminster during the 'great stink' of 1853. This crisis led to the construction of the magnificent Victorian sewer system, on which London still largely depends.

Sewers also replaced the need for the cesspits which were often found on individual properties. Lined with a variety of materials – stone, ⑤ wood and wattle in the early periods and cattle horns or brick ⑥ from the sixteenth century onwards – these cesspits provided a place for the disposal of all kinds of waste for a great many Londoners. As a result they often contain a wealth of finds, as well as animal bones, seeds and traces of parasites. Environmental archaeologists can examine these remains to study the diet and health of the owners. Clearly the cesspits were evil-smelling and unpleasant, and even when valuable items such as gold rings were accidentally dropped into them, their owners were understandably reluctant to retrieve them. Sometimes the pits had latrines attached, but often chamber pots ⑦ were emptied straight into them. One remarkably intimate find was a three-person toilet seat excavated from the banks of the River Fleet. ⑧

Many Londoners simply threw their rubbish into pits in their own yards and gardens, ⑨ allowing archaeologists to build up a picture of individuals' lifestyles. Today our rubbish is taken away and the link with our houses is broken.

This 12th-century dug-out drain, running south into the Thames, had a flap valve at its riverward end which was still in working order when excavated

7

8

4

5

Above middle The chalk walls of a massive medieval cesspit associated with an important property at Plantation Place, City; **Right** An 18th-century cesspit behind houses fronting on to Spital Square

6

9

Left The wattle lining of this 12th-century waste pit is typical of many found in London

Above The Roman City wall is still visible in places, as here at London Wall, where crenellations were added in the 15th century; **Right** Excavating part of the southern wall of the Roman Cripplegate fort

Left A military stamp depicting an eagle is visible on this boot sole; **Below** Reconstruction of Roman scale armour (in grey) based on surviving fragments found at a site on the Roman waterfront; the small sections of metal sheet were wired together and sewn to a fabric backing

London's defences

Londinium's first defences were built in the early second century AD, when the Romans constructed a fort in the north-western corner of the city. ❶ Professor W. F. Grimes discovered it in the 1950s when he was excavating bomb-damaged buildings in the area. Laid out in the typical playing-card shape, with gates located centrally on each side, the fort covered an area of about 5 hectares and was surrounded by a stone wall. Inside were the remains of several stone buildings, presumably barrack blocks, fronting on to gravel roads. ❷ A legionary attachment was probably stationed at the fort, but it seems to have gone out of use by the end of the third century.

Around AD 200 a stone wall about 3 km long and 4 m high, topped with battlements and a walkway, was built around the landward

side of the city, linking up with the fort. ❸ The wall was punctuated by five gates – Ludgate, Newgate, Aldersgate, Bishopsgate and Aldgate – all still nodal points in the modern road network. It is not clear why such a substantial wall was built, as no serious military threats to southern England are known at this time. It may have been erected simply for civic reasons, perhaps in response to an edict issued by the Emperor Septimius Severus (AD 193–211), who arrived in Britain during 208 to campaign in Scotland. Whatever its purpose, it must certainly have impressed the inhabitants of the time.

Later on, as military threats to London's security increased, the river frontage was defended by a continuous wall. During the late fourth century a series of bastions was added to the eastern section of the city

wall and a wide ditch was dug beyond the walls on the landward side.

When the Roman city was re-occupied by the Saxons in the late ninth century the walls and gates were refortified. In around 1200 stone bastions were added to the western section of the defences and the line of the walls was extended westwards to the River Fleet. A broad ditch flanked the wall, which served as an unofficial rubbish dump and was left to silt up. ❹ Items found in it include large quantities of discarded everyday objects, including leather shoes, belt fittings, knife scabbards, ❺ wooden vessels, pottery jugs and bowls. In the sixteenth century this ditch was no longer required for defence and it was filled in. In many ways the walls acted as a barrier to London's expansion and were one of the main causes for massive overcrowding.

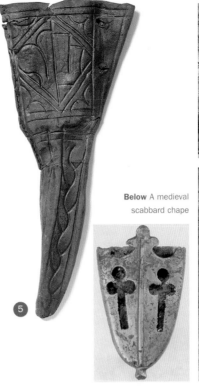

Below A medieval scabbard chape

Above A bombard shot made of Portland stone found in marshy ground opposite the Tower of London, and possibly fired from it in Tudor times as a practice shot

Two castles were built by the Normans to defend the settlement and to serve as a reminder to the inhabitants of who their new masters were. One was Baynard's Castle, now long gone; at the other side of the City was the Tower of London. **6** William the Conqueror built the Tower's massive stone keep in the 1070s and additions were made by many of the English kings over the centuries. It has had many uses – palace, prison and even zoo. Archaeologists have discovered the site of earlier curtain walls and gates, now demolished, and have also excavated within the moat.

The last major defensive wall built around London was constructed in the early 1640s to protect the capital during the English Civil War. **7** London was by then a much larger city and the wall, consisting of an earth embankment with 'star-shaped' forts in the latest style, was sited far out from the medieval defences. It was soon demolished, however, and nothing now survives, although a small fort, perhaps for practice, was found by archaeologists in the Tower of London's artillery ground in Spitalfields. **8**

7 Plan of London's defensive ring of forts and ditches constructed during the 1640s Civil War period

Left Detail from a 16th-century map showing target practice within the Artillery Ground, with archaeological evidence in the form of musket balls and lead shot

Left The boundary wall around the Artillery Ground, where the Master Gunner of England lived

Industry

In addition to being a trading emporium for centuries, London has also been a thriving manufacturing centre, producing goods for use both at home and abroad. Many of those trades and industries have left traces which archaeologists can find beneath the ground in London.

① A fragment of Neolithic pottery from Southwark

Below A complete mortarium (mixing bowl), with a gritted interior designed to aid the mixing and grinding of herbs and other foods. This vessel was imported from north Gaul and carries the stamp of the potter who made it; potters in London copied examples such as this; **Right** Excavating a mortarium found in the debris of a Roman building

②

A dog's paw-print in a Roman tile from excavations at Regis House

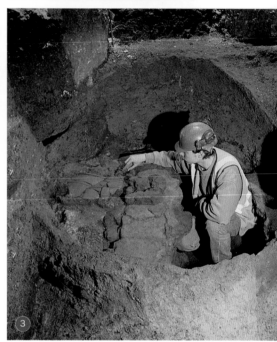

③

Pottery

The Romans brought with them a very different cuisine from that familiar to the native Britons. And along with the new ingredients also came a highly distinctive range of ceramic vessels for storing, preparing and serving food. Roman methods of pottery production were also very distinct. Instead of making vessels by hand, as most Iron Age (pre-Roman) potters did, ① the Romans used a potter's wheel to shape and finish vessels. This facilitated the production of large quantities of highly standardised vessels. New kiln technology was also introduced by the Romans, allowing large numbers of vessels to be fired at one time and giving potters greater control over the conditions in the kiln, which determine the colour and hardness of the vessels.

The earliest evidence for pottery production in London comes from the south of the City, where a group of 'wasters' was found dating to the earliest phase of occupation of London, about AD 50–55. A waster is a vessel which was damaged or spoilt in some way during firing and is therefore discarded by the potter. A full range of Roman vessel types was produced in London, including jars, beakers, bowls, flagons and mixing bowls called mortaria – the distinctive mixing and grinding vessel that was essential to Roman cooking. ②

A selection of vessels found at the important 2nd-century kiln site at Moorgate. Potters who worked at the kilns can be identified from stamps on the mortaria (mixing bowls) and included Lucius, Valentinus and Maximus

⑤

Above Two Roman oil lamps from Moorgate, both showing the remains of the mica coating originally applied to give them a metallic look

Above middle Experimental kiln constructed close to the site of the Roman pottery kilns at Highgate Woods; **Above right** Fresh from the kiln, the result of an experimental firing; **Above** Roman pottery of Highgate Woods manufacture

Recent excavations in Moorgate have produced our best evidence for a thriving Roman pottery industry in Londinium in the first half of the second century AD. Archaeologists were surprised to discover five kilns, ③ and the large quantities of wasters ④ show that the potters were producing a great variety of vessels. These range from highly burnished (polished) and decorated tablewares to large storage vessels and mortaria which would have been used in the kitchen. ⑤ Many of the table wares were finished with a thin coat of the mineral mica, giving them a gold or bronze finish in imitation of metal vessels. ⑥ Before this discovery, evidence for pottery production had been scarce: several kilns were found during the rebuilding of St Paul's Cathedral in the seventeenth century and another kiln was discovered nearby in 1961. The associated pottery indicates a late first- to early second-century date.

Archaeologists have located a major pottery industry to the north-west of the Roman city, clustered along Watling Street at Brockley Hill, Verulamium, Radlett and Bricket Wood. Potters here produced mainly white wares, which dominated the London market in the late first and early second centuries. Kilns have also been excavated in Highgate Woods, just north of the City, which were producing greyware jars, bowls and beakers. ⑦ These included distinctive highly burnished 'poppyhead' beakers decorated with applied dots. ⑧

Evidence for pottery manufacture is lacking in London itself and at the nearby production centres for the later Roman period. It seems instead that London's pottery was supplied by the large out-of-town industries, such as those in Oxfordshire and the Nene Valley.

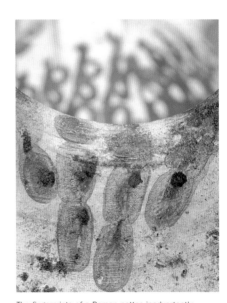

The fingerprints of a Roman potter, inadvertently applied inside the rim of a vessel during its decoration

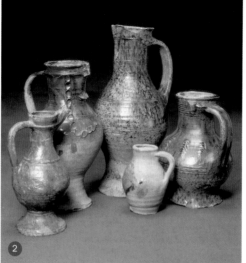

Above 'Westminster' floor tiles – named after Westminster Abbey where they were first recognised – were being mass produced by London tilemakers by the 1260s. These examples can still be seen in the chapel at Lambeth Palace

Above middle Medieval jugs made in Kingston; **Left** Anthropomorphic jugs; **Above and below** Three complete ceramic late 16th-century watering cans, found in a well in Westminster

From the late eleventh century onwards, London was a focus of technological innovation and a melting pot of influences and fashions in the ceramic industries. Potters were making all manner of wares, from everyday kitchen and storage vessels to highly decorative and expensive tablewares, as well as ceramic building materials such as roof, wall and floor tiles. ❶

A series of far-reaching advances in pottery technology spread from the capital to the surrounding area and beyond. The introduction of glazing and the use of the potter's wheel at the end of the eleventh century revolutionised pottery manufacture and gave rise to an industry of major importance. Produced from local clays at centres archaeologists have yet to excavate, London-made red earthenwares flourished from the twelfth to mid fourteenth centuries. Reviving again in the fifteenth century, they provided the majority of household and industrial wares into the nineteenth century. ❷ Redwares were made at Kingston upon Thames and Cheam in south London in the late fifteenth and sixteenth centuries, and later at Woolwich and Deptford in south-east London.

A major medieval ceramic industry producing green-glazed whitewares was centred on Kingston upon Thames. Archaeologists excavating kilns there have unearthed huge quantities of discarded waste, the results of firing and production accidents. ❸ Between the mid thirteenth and early fifteenth centuries potters made a wide range of kitchen and serving vessels, as well as metalworking crucibles,

One of the most significant developments in London's early post-medieval ceramic industries was the introduction of tin-glazed ware, or 'delftware', following the arrival of potters from Antwerp who set up in Aldgate in 1571. The operation closed in 1615 and the industry moved south of the Thames, to Southwark. From 1618, Christian Wilhelm's Pickleherring factory was making highly decorative Chinese-inspired wares. One such pot, made in 1627, was found by chance by archaeologists watching a tunnel being dug, deep beneath the road outside of the Houses of Parliament. ❹ Large amounts of tin-glazed ware waste from

Left A delftware bottle painted with blue and white bird-on-rock decoration, with the date, 1627, beneath the handle; **Above** The remarkable diversity of household tableware disposed of in a cesspit at Norfolk House; **Right** The base of one of five kilns at Doulton's 19th-century stoneware manufactory in Lambeth. The flues had been backfilled with whole pots and kiln debris, including shelves which retained splashes of glaze and circular shadows left after the removal of the fired products

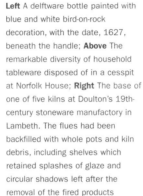

Above Delftware tiles

5 Two examples of Limehouse waster porcelain sherds, produced in the mid 1740s

the Rotherhithe factory – both unglazed, biscuit-fired wares and twice-fired, finished pottery – include stacks of vessels that had fused together in the kiln. Archaeologists have excavated other potteries in south London – in Lambeth, Wapping and Mortlake – which closed in the early nineteenth century when production of tin-glazed ware in London ceased.

Stoneware was not successfully manufactured in England on a commercial basis until 1672, when John Dwight received a patent for the sole right of production in England. This innovation had far-reaching effects, and after the patent had expired stoneware factories sprang up all over the country, with several major producers in London. Dwight was one of the great pioneers of

English pottery and his failed experiments in making true porcelain after the Chinese model have been recovered from the Fulham Pottery. It was not until the middle of the eighteenth century that a breakthrough was made, and London was once more in the forefront of developments, with early porcelain production taking place at Chelsea (1743–44) and Limehouse, where archaeologists found a kiln and ceramic waste. 5 The pothouse there was short-lived, opening in 1744–45 and closing in 1748, probably because the porcelain was still at an experimental stage. Nevertheless, an astonishing range of household wares was recovered, decorated in under-glaze blue, heralding the wider development of porcelain manufacture, both in London and beyond.

③ **Above** Careful excavation of one of many decorated bone Saxon spindle whorls found during the redevelopment of the Royal Opera House; **Left** Decorated spindle whorls

④ **Left** Clay loom-weights, used to keep the vertical threads taut on the loom, have been found on many sites in Saxon Lundenwic; **Above** Reconstruction of a Saxon loom

Tanning, textiles & leatherworking

Above Saxon bone needles

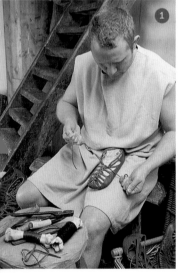

①  ②

Leather survives well in waterlogged conditions and huge quantities have been excavated by archaeologists at waterfront sites. No production sites for Roman London have yet been identified, but it is certain that leather goods were being made in the Walbrook area, as large amounts of leather artefacts and waste have been found, as well as a number of leather-working tools. It is not yet known whether the Roman leatherworking industry operated through a limited number of larger production centres or through smaller, possibly itinerant, workshops. ① It is clear, however, that the fashions in the footwear of Roman Londoners changed. ② Shoes found include finely decorated slippers for indoor female attire and large outdoor boots with heavily nailed soles, probably worn by soldiers.

Other leather artefacts are less common, but include tent panels (some of which may have been for military use), satchel-type bags, fragments from saddles and decorative pieces that were probably applied to furnishings.

Evidence for both spinning and weaving has been found in Roman London. Spindle whorls ③ and loom-weights ④ – made from stone, bone or even reworked fragments of pottery – are frequent finds. Spindles are less common, probably due to their more fragile nature, but they do survive occasionally. The many needles, both bone and metal, that are found on Roman sites in London are evidence for the working of textiles – one unusual tool was used to produce braids or ribbons.

The particularly evil-smelling leather industries were banished to the fringes of the city during the Middle Ages – notably Bermondsey, south of the Thames. Pits uncovered at several sites in these areas were probably connected with tanning, and a large curved iron blade of the 1500s may have been used to separate the usable hide from the rest of the dead animal.

Direct evidence for shoe-making and leatherworking in the medieval period, as for the Roman period, has proved elusive, but awls and specialised blades that were

Below Medieval leather craftsman at work, in a 15th-century illustration; such scenes would have been repeated around London, and are reflected in the naming of Leather Lane; **Right** These superbly crafted shoes and ankle-boots were among a large number found in 10th-century cesspits in the middle of the City, and display a number of styles, some with decorative stitching and embroidery; **Below middle** The discovery of a well-preserved leather shoe from waterlogged deposits

Left Cloth seals. The cloth manufacturer was identifiable by the design of the stamp; **Above** Drawing of part of a leather jerkin with detail of cuts, button holes and other decoration, well preserved in waterlogged deposits in Southwark

probably used to cut out the leather have been found. Once again, archaeologists digging along the waterfront have found large amounts of leather, including worn-out shoes, 5 some of which had plainly been cut for recycling, presumably to patch other footwear.

Simple spindle whorls are evidence of the large domestic effort that Londoners of all classes contributed to thread production. Fine needles were probably used for both domestic and commercial embroidery.

The commercial finishing of textiles, particularly dyeing, is evident from the thousands of lead seals 6 found along the waterfront and on the sites of clothdrying areas called tentergrounds, which were used to regulate the industry from the late medieval period to the early nineteenth century. Large groups of seals recovered from the Thames include examples from a series issued by the Dyers' Guild in the seventeenth century, which specify woad, cochineal or combinations of colourants. Their distribution seems to

conform to areas where riverside dye houses were located. 7 Seals from textiles woven in some twenty English counties as well as from continental imports confirm and supplement documentary evidence for an extensive range of sources for the cloth coming into London.

Above top Medieval awls used in the working of leather; **Above** An 18th-century drainage channel in Southwark. Skinning marks and butchery exhibited by the horse, cattle and sheep bones found in it suggest that the channel was used by the local tanning industry; **Left** Medieval dyers at work on the riverside

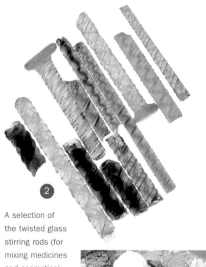

A selection of the twisted glass stirring rods (for mixing medicines and cosmetics) found at Regis House

Above The scorched base of a small furnace belonging to a glass workshop within a 1st-century Roman quayside warehouse at Regis House; **Right** A Roman moile – waste glass from the end of a blowing iron

Left A massive dump of waste glass found on the site of the amphitheatre was carefully collected for future analysis; **Above** An experimental furnace based upon the Roman evidence from London

Glassworking

Twenty-five years ago, very little evidence existed for glassworking in London. Now, however, we have a wealth of information from the Roman period up to the present day.

Many glass vessels, for everyday use, were made in Roman London, but more luxurious vessels such as the Italian millefiori bowl from which this fragment comes, were imported from elsewhere in the Roman Empire

Examples of beautiful Roman glass vessels used as grave goods to accompany the dead, from graves excavated to the east of the City; burial goods such as these are often the best-preserved examples of their kind

Excavations at Regis House near London Bridge have confirmed that glassblowing was introduced by itinerant glassworkers shortly after the destruction of the Roman town by Queen Boudica in AD 60. Archaeologists excavated a warehouse there ❶ which was used for the manufacture of small bottles, drinking cups and stirring rods for mixing drinks. ❷

A number of other sites have provided evidence of glassworking though all of them were recycling existing glass rather than manufacturing new. Most important by far is a dump of glass weighing 50 kg found during the excavation of the amphitheatre at the Guildhall. ❸ Archaeologists discovered a residential and light-industrial zone to the east of the amphitheatre, in use between about AD 120 and 130. For reasons which we may never know, this mass of broken glass – known as cullet – containing more

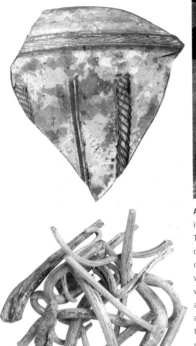

Above left The glassworks at Broad Street were heavily influenced by styles from overseas, especially Venice. This fragment of a drinking vessel has Venetian-style decoration but the poorer quality of the glass is typical of London products; **Left** The manufacture of glass vessels produces a variety of waste, such as these threads and droplets; **Above** An archaeologist examines the heavily burnt brick base of a 17th/18th-century glass kiln from the Bear Gardens glasshouse on Bankside

Above top A view down the flue of the Vauxhall Bridge furnace. The pots which contained the glass would have been placed on the brick side walls; **Above** A fragment from the bottom of a pot with 1-inch-thick walls, used to hold the molten glass. This one shattered in the furnace, the glass flowing through the crack on the left; **Left** Many bottles made in the Vauxhall factory were commissioned with personalised seals, such as this, stamped on their sides

than 100,000 fragments from over 2000 vessels and many thousands of fragments of waste from the glassworker's trade, was discarded and not reused. It is of international importance because the dump contained a wide range of vessels broken and collected for reuse, providing us with an exceptional insight into the variety and types of glassware in general use in the province of Britannia at the time of the Emperors Trajan and Hadrian.

A generation later, around the middle of the second century, glassworkers had set up their furnaces further north in the city, around the Copthall Avenue and Moorgate area, near the city wall. Excavations there have produced some of the best evidence for glass furnaces. Although very fragmentary, they have led to a programme of experimentation that has allowed modern glass researchers to recreate full-scale working furnaces. ④

A small number of nationally important glassware-production sites and waste dumps from the post-medieval period have also now been excavated in London. The capital was the location of the only certain crystal-glass (cristallo) production sites in England, so the evidence from these sites is of particular interest.

Two groups of waste material have been investigated which originated from the Broad Street factory operated from the early seventeenth century by Sir Robert Mansell. His glassworkers were working in both traditional green and the much finer colourless glass known as 'crystal'. Kilos of waste from a range of his products have been found, including rods of decorative white and blue glass for applying to beer beakers and other prestigious vessels of colourless glass.

On the site of the factory ⑤ named after the Bear Gardens once situated in the area, and dating from a couple of generations later, archaeologists found further groups of waste green and crystal glass. The factory produced a range of vessels in a richer blue and its wares include some relatively unusual forms as well as fragments of another recently developed line: plate glass for mirrors.

Another factory, dating from the early 1700s and located south of Vauxhall Bridge, seems, from the material recovered, to have been more limited in its production, relying heavily on green-glass wine bottles. ⑥ The remains of the factory here are of key significance to the history of development in England of the furnace cone. ⑦

Above Metalworking in the Bronze Age. Metal was first worked in around 3000 BC. Copper was the first metal to be used by prehistoric peoples, shortly followed by the working of bronze

A fragment of mould for a bronze sword or spear blade found in a Late Bronze Age well near Heathrow

Above Three lead ingots discovered at Regis House. They are each 600 mm (2 Roman feet) long and weigh about 150–70 lbs. Lead was one of the most important metals mined in Britain, not least because the refining of lead ore was the only source of silver in the Roman world and silver was vital for the production of coinage; Below Part of a late Roman stone mould, probably for the production of pewter plates, with a rim decorated with running animals, perhaps dogs

Metalworking

A wide range of evidence for the working of both precious and non-precious metals has been uncovered in Roman London. Iron was smelted in large quantities in Kent and Sussex to the south of London, as well as elsewhere in Britain. Most excavations in London produce quantities of iron smithing slag, but the actual workshops are less frequently found. Smithing hearth bottoms and hammerscale (microscopic debris) recovered from several sites show that metalworking took place around the Walbrook stream on the north bank of the Thames, and also in Southwark on the south bank. These areas have also produced copper alloy waste and ceramic crucibles for smelting, as well as evidence for the recycling of copper alloy artefacts.

We also have evidence for the production of objects in lead and tin alloy. Lead was mined in Wales and the west of England and was mixed with tin to produce pewter.

One of the most remarkable discoveries by archaeologists in recent years was a group of three lead 'pigs' or ingots buried beneath the floor of a warehouse dating to the late first century AD near London Bridge. All three bore the official stamp of Vespasian and originally came from the Mendip Hills in Somerset. Pewter vessels were produced in the later Roman period, from the mid third to the early fifth centuries AD, although evidence for their production in London is limited. The discovery of the base of a stack of stone moulds for making dishes as well as part of a limestone mould for making pewter plates indicates that such items were being made in London. Crucibles with traces of gold show that this metal too was being worked in the city.

Left Some of over 500 Roman coin moulds discovered at London Wall, the equipment of a forger during the 3rd century

Left Roman tiles reused as moulds to manufacture small bronze ingots; these are extremely rare in Saxon London; **Above right** This chunk of lead alloy waste (known as a 'litharge cake') had collected in the base of a hearth during the process of silver-working during the 11th century on the site at Poultry

Left A complete Roman copper alloy cauldron discovered within a well

For the medieval period archaeologists have found abundant traces of the mass production of cast buckles, brooches, mounts and rings, all in copper alloy. Furnaces and clay moulds discovered near the Guildhall are rare survivals, showing that tens of similar items were cast at one time. **3** Elsewhere, sheet mounts were cut out by metalworkers and shaped in individual, labour-intensive operations. Large cauldrons and bells of relatively simple form were made in single castings. Openwork copper alloy sleeves were made in the fourteenth century for composite knife handles of bone, jet and amber. In the sixteenth century pins were given wound-wire heads and filed while held steady on specially adapted animal-bone rests (called pinner's bones), a low-tech manufacture seen at several sites across London. **4** And in the seventeenth century, components for copper alloy candlesticks were separately cast and assembled later.

Pewter accessories, some very ornate, were cast in stone moulds. Wasters from this process include a brooch designed to be decorated with several green-glass stones, only one of which was fixed in place during production when the metal failed to flow properly.

A site in Bermondsey produced a series of sixteenth-century knives, heavy-duty washers and a key, all unfinished. Some were discarded during manufacture because they accidentally broke on the anvil, while others were left incomplete for reasons that remain unknown. Occasional hints of the working of precious metals are usually confined to waste products from refining and crucibles, but a mould made of cuttlefish bone for studs in the form of an ornate letter 'M', probably of silver, survives from the fifteenth century.

3

Above Some waste material from cast iron production at Guildhall; **Below left** Drawing of a 14th-century ceramic mould for making buckles; **Below right** An X-ray through an otherwise shapeless lump of corrosion from the site at Guildhall shows three copper alloy belt-buckles joined together

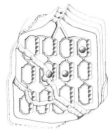

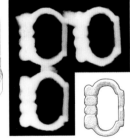

Above left Two pinner's bones; **Above and right** Medieval metalworking crucibles made in Kingston-upon-Thames

A Tudor lead tankard from excavations at London Bridge

London's trade

Left This hoard of 43 gold coins had been intentionally buried in a purse inside a small box; it represents about 10 years' pay for an infantry soldier (Plantation House); Above left Many Roman carpentry tools, some remarkably like those in use today, have been found in London, especially in the Walbrook streambed; some examples have been reconstructed by the Museum of London; Above right A late 1st-century metalsmith's or furniture-maker's shop, with floor joists visible after removal of the original plank floor

Shops & markets

From Roman times onwards London has been remarkable for its vibrant commercial character.

The location of Roman London at the hub of Britain's distribution system – combining river, port, road and marketplace – meant that the city was a bustling emporium. Money could be made from trade and from associated services, such as transport, storage and tax collection. However, much of the physical evidence of trade and commerce is ephemeral or difficult to distinguish from the activities of daily life.

Above A rare miniature amphora from the 2nd century. It may have been used as a stopper or unguent jar

Left Reconstructed scene of a bakery; Below left The excavation of a double-oven dating to the 1st century in the heart of the City

An early Roman roadside shop in the heart of the City

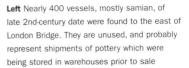

Excavations suggest that the majority of shops and businesses were located in private houses. Large residential buildings might include workshops as well as premises for providers of services, such as doctors or pharmacists, and bars and restaurants. Houses used by carpenters, **2** metalworkers **3** and other craftsmen have been found lining the main roads, and industries that required a copious supply of water had begun to cluster in yards along the Walbrook stream. Bakeries sold bread and cakes direct to the public from adjoining shops, as in one roadside building near the Walbrook. **4** Shops specialising in the sale of household goods and other consumer products were established before the Boudican revolt of AD 60. **5**

As in all Roman towns, London's central market lay in its forum. **6** It was a meeting place for a variety of transactions and many people would gather there each day to take part in the public business. A bustling precinct located at the junction of the two main streets, its buildings housed the council and courts. In over thirty years of investigations archaeologists have found many of the forum walls, a short distance from the main port on the Thames. Street markets were also important commercial centres, where butchers, barbers and other businesses would have carried out their trade. London also had more formal colonnaded shopping streets, such as one excavated by archaeologists along the approach to the southern bridgehead in Southwark.

Shopkeepers and workers lived and slept on their premises or rented small rooms nearby – convenient, given that the working day began at sunrise. The economy was sufficiently developed for most households to have surplus income to buy many of their daily staples, although people in the town may also have grown some of their own food. Basic foods such as bread were produced locally, and exotic imports were available from shops and stalls. Cellar storehouses, **7** such as one found on Bishopsgate, may have been either domestic or commercial in scale. A waterfront timber warehouse in Southwark and masonry storehouses found in the city near the bridge at Pudding Lane **8** represent just some of Roman London's port and market facilities.

The volume of trade and commerce declined after the mid second century as the economy of Britannia became less dependent on London and fewer goods passed through the port. The town continued to contain a range of shops and businesses, many of them housed in basic timber buildings, but they were now fewer in number. Some of these properties had been maintained through successive rebuildings since the town's formative years, and even gained expensive additions, suggesting that some merchants at least continued to flourish and perhaps expanded their long-established businesses.

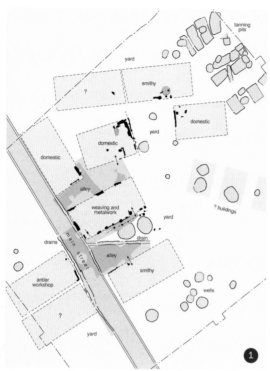

Interpretive plan of the urban landscape of the mid 8th century revealed by excavations at the Royal Opera House

Above Reconstruction of the marketplace near Poultry in about 1100; **Left** A copper alloy cow bell found trodden into the late Saxon hollow-way leading to the market place at Poultry; **Below** Saxo-Norman coins dating to the 11th and 12th centuries

Above Part of the 16th-century Agas map, with trades in the City indicated by street names (Milk Street, Ironmonger Lane, Wood Street, Bread Street)

As in the Roman period, many of Saxon London's shops were on the ground floor of ordinary houses. The distribution of finds from excavations in Lundenwic, particularly in and around Covent Garden, shows that the houses, sometimes arranged around courtyards, were occupied by a variety of tradespeople. **1** Blacksmiths, boneworkers, metalworkers and weavers worked side-by-side with other industries such as butchers and bakers. In the medieval period this changed, with individual trades clustering together in certain parts of the city, so that, for example, clothworkers practised their trade close to the river and dyers were found in the north part of the city.

Beach markets were one feature of trade in the re-established city in the tenth century.

Boats would offload their wares and sell them on the foreshore either to local traders or direct to the inhabitants. One example has been found by archaeologists near the earliest dock at Queenhithe. As the settlement of London expanded, a new market grew up next to the Walbrook. Enclosures for livestock were erected in a central area, surrounded by buildings in which the actual business of buying and selling may have been carried out. **2** During the twelfth century this market developed into an area occupied by wealthy merchants and financiers, with small shops along the street frontages.

One of London's principal medieval market buildings was Leadenhall, **3** built in 1439 by the city authorities in the heart of the

city over the site of the old Roman forum. It consisted of four ranges of stone buildings around a central courtyard. Archaeologists have found some of its walls still remarkably well preserved, allowing its appearance in its heyday to be reconstructed. Poultry, food stuffs, grain, eggs, butter and cheese were sold on the arcaded ground floor, while the upper two floors were used for the storage of grain to keep it dry and safe from pests.

Some markets were seasonal, such as the October Fair held held in the precincts of Westminster Abbey. Itinerant traders who followed fairs around the country would sell their wares alongside the wealthy merchants who lived in the fine painted stone houses.

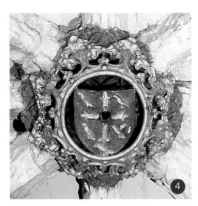

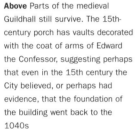

Above Parts of the medieval Guildhall still survive. The 15th-century porch has vaults decorated with the coat of arms of Edward the Confessor, suggesting perhaps that even in the 15th century the City believed, or perhaps had evidence, that the foundation of the building went back to the 1040s

Left Stacks of early 19th-century pedestal-based ointment pots from Mortlake High Street

Above A view over two rooms, separated by internal partition walls made of chalk blocks, of Blackwell Hall, described in its heyday as the greatest woollen cloth market in medieval England; **Left** An unused cloth seal from excavations at Guildhall. The central rivet would have been pressed flat when it was attached to a cloth by the authorities to certify quality and indicate that appropriate taxes had been levied on the cloth

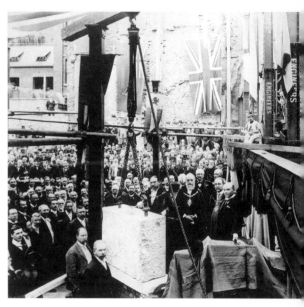

Above Laying the foundation stone of the Baltic Mercantile and Shipping Exchange in 1900. The Baltic Company, founded in the 16th century and based in the financial centre of the City, specialised in trading naval stores, tallow and grain. The new headquarters reflected the importance of the company, with marble-clad walls and columns, and three handpainted glass domes in the high ceiling; **Below** The market at Smithfield is the last to remain on its medieval site

London's government was based on the guilds which controlled the various trades. Each had its own guild building, but they all met to govern the city at the Guildhall, an enormous complex which was certainly in existence by 1220. ❹ Aldermen were in charge of government, while the mayor and sheriffs dispensed justice. The hall lay on the north side of a yard which was surrounded by a stone wall, entered through a gatehouse. Structures excavated in the yard include a large stone chapel built in 1299, a stone building where the Common Council perhaps met and, on the east side, Blackwell Hall, the principal woollen cloth market in England. ❺ The Guildhall itself was rebuilt between 1411 and 1430 by John Croxton and still stands today, although damaged during the Great Fire of 1666 and the Second World War. It was raised above the contemporary level and now overlies vaulted crypts.

As production became more centralised to meet the needs of the rapidly increasing numbers of Londoners, so market buildings became larger and better organised. Several new ones were established in the seventeenth century or later, including Spitalfields and Covent Garden for fruit and vegetables, Billingsgate for fish and Smithfield ❻ for meat. Many were rebuilt in the nineteenth century, while in the latter part of the twentieth century most moved out of central London.

Above The interior of a timber-floored early Roman quayside warehouse under excavation at Regis House; **Right** An impressively preserved part of London's 1st-century quay, looking north, with a 2nd-century open drain cutting through it

The docks

London's development and prosperity are inextricably bound up with its waterfront and its status as a major trading centre.

A large, nearly complete amphora from the Rhone Valley found in a Roman building which may have been a warehouse for storing the goods shipped into Southwark

From its Roman origins through to the post-Victorian decline of the enclosed dock system, London's port was always the foundation of the city's commercial success and provided employment and financial reward for a high percentage of its population.

At its height in the late first and second centuries, the Roman port required major storage facilities. Large numbers of warehouses were built, ① often with stone walls and timber floors, which were divided into individual units. Extensive mudbrick buildings ② excavated by archaeologists near London Bridge were used for storage and light industry; they may also have been the site of a quayside marketplace and one building was used as a glassworker's shop for a time. It was in one of these quayside buildings that three 'British' lead ingots ③ bearing the stamp of Vespasian (AD 69–79) were found. In the third century a defensive

stone wall was built, effectively separating the waterfront from the city, and the port declined.

Buildings in the city indicate central planning and probably public investment, with premises rented out to individuals. In Southwark, by contrast, the dockside was probably operated on a private basis. One small building is thought to have been a private merchant's warehouse. ④ Dated to AD 152–53 by tree-ring analysis, it was in use for only a few years.

We have practically no archaeological evidence for Saxon dockside activity in Lundenwic, although the Venerable Bede, writing in the early eighth century, described it as a thriving port. As yet, few excavations have been possible in the areas where most evidence might be found. After the resettlement of the walled Roman city in the late ninth century, the port once more

Right The inlet at Queenhithe, the City's first medieval dock, is still visible today
⑤

④

Left A well-preserved timber warehouse in Southwark. Lying close to the river and sunk into the ground, it would have offered cool and damp conditions ideal for the storage of wine and food; **Above left** Reconstruction of the timber warehouse; **Above** Detail of a barrel used to import wine to Roman London from the German frontier. The branded stamp CEGFIC across the barrel's bung was perhaps intended to prevent tampering during shipment

⑥
A political cartoon of 1757 shows the busy character of the London waterfront

became central to the growth of London. Queenhithe and Billingsgate were the main trading docks, as they were throughout the medieval period. Queenhithe, ⑤ upstream of London Bridge, mainly handled cargoes from inland, particularly corn, while Billingsgate, downstream of the bridge, catered for international trade. Naturally, these two landing-places became the focus for dockside activity and each had access to inland markets. Land around the quays was reclaimed and intensively occupied, initially by timber buildings which were later replaced in stone. To operate successfully, both docks also required open areas on the landward side, called Romeland. Later in the medieval period colonnaded arcades served as waterfront markets.

The Romeland was surrounded by warehousing, workshops and houses. One thirteenth-century merchant's house next

to Queenhithe fronted on to a lane that led down to the dock. It had a stone basement which still preserved the remains of securely barred windows to protect the owner's stock from thieves. Such cellars were common all along the waterfront.

Other waterfront institutions in the City included the Steelyard at Dowgate, first recorded in 1170. This was a dock and guildhall set up by Cologne merchants which later became the centre for trading cloth. To the east was the Custom House, which regulated international trade. Dating from 1382, it was built on reclaimed land.

The ever-increasing volume of trade outgrew the City in the seventeenth and eighteenth centuries, ⑥ and the Port of London expanded eastwards into the Isle of Dogs and beyond, eventually becoming the largest in the world in the nineteenth century.

Part of the 'banana' wall at West India Docks, Canary Wharf, built in about 1800 to a special design to accommodate the shape of ships' hulls. The sloping wall and its angled timber supporting frame can be clearly seen

1

Just a few of the 1100 rotary quernstones recovered from Poultry, a 1st-century site in the city, the largest assemblage to be retrieved from anywhere in the Roman Empire. The majority were made of lava and had been imported from Germany. Many contained hoppers, feed pipes, spindle holes and handle slots. Wear patterns indicate that the querns had been used prior to disposal, probably in a nearby mill or bakery. Cobbled surfaces were frequently constructed of broken quernstones

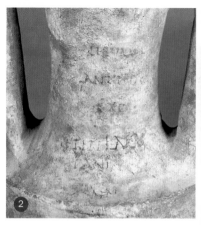

Amphorae – Roman storage jars – were used for transporting commodities such as black olives in syrup, wine, fish sauce and alum (used for fixing dyes to textiles). An exceptional find from Winchester Palace was an amphora imported from the Mediterranean with contents that included Spanish mackerel bones. A faint painted Latin inscription states that 'Lucius Tettius Africanus supplies the finest fish sauce from Antibes'

Imported commodities

3

Above A sherd from a South Gaulish samian ware bowl depicting a hare; **Below** One of a group of unused samian vessels recovered from a Roman shop destroyed in the Boudican revolt of AD 60

Goods imported into Roman London

Roman London was a thriving commercial centre but it could not survive on its own produce alone. Goods and raw materials came from all parts of the Empire, including other parts of Britain, to meet the demand for items essential for maintaining the Roman way of life.

Exotic ingredients, as well as the means of preparing foods, came from abroad. Millstones and quernstones (from hand mills), for grinding flour, came from the Mayen area of Germany. **1** Olive oil, important both in cooking and for lighting, was carried in amphorae from the Mediterranean. Spain was an important source of oil and also produced garum, a fermented fish sauce used as a seasoning. Painted inscriptions recorded the contents of the amphorae, which might be olives, dried fruit or wine. **2** German wine was imported in barrels made of silver fir, some of which were later reused to line wells or cisterns. The wood was also used to make writing tablets, both for letters and to record commercial transactions.

Fashionable ceramic tablewares came from Gaul, where glossy redwares (samian) were mass produced, either plain or decorated with floral, mythological, hunting or gladiatorial scenes. **3** As local industries

Below Roman potters often stamped a maker's mark on their wares – this example shows the stamp of Mercator, a 2nd-century potter from Gaul

4 A necked bowl with stamped decoration from kilns in the Oxfordshire region, dated AD 340–400+. The style was an attempt to copy the imported samian vessels

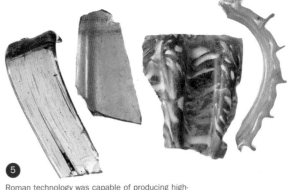

A group of pottery recovered from a well in Southwark. The well-preserved hunt-scene vessels in the foreground are from 2nd-century Cologne, while the other vessels are all early 3rd-century Romano-British

5 Roman technology was capable of producing high-quality glass vessels and many different types were imported to London. **Left** Glass beaker, decorated with applied blue glass blobs, made in the Rhineland in the 3rd century. It was found in a burial in the eastern cemetery of Roman London; **Above** Handles and other fragments of vessels such as these give an indication of the richness of colour and style of imported glass

became established, pottery was supplied from other parts of Britain, including Verulamium (St Albans), the Nene Valley, Surrey and Oxfordshire. **4** Italy provided bronze tablewares, while luxury glassware came from first-century workshops in the Rhineland and the Mediterranean. **5** In the later Roman period distinctive bottles and flagons were among imports from Gaul and Germany.

Oil lamps in copper alloy and pottery were imported from Italy and Gaul in the first and second centuries. Decorative marbles for building and interior decoration were transported from quarries in Turkey, Greece, Italy, North Africa and France. Sculptures of the gods came from the continent and, on a smaller scale, ceramic (pipe-clay) figurines travelled from Gaul. Fine bronze figurines came to the province from abroad, as did an oil flask in the form of Bacchus. A figurine of a sphinx may be from the lid of a vessel. **6** Personal items, particularly

jewellery, are often dug up by archaeologists in London. Emerald, for necklaces, came from Egypt and amber from the Baltic. Enamelled brooches were made in the north-west provinces.

Other parts of Britain provided a wide range of goods in addition to pottery, either to be consumed by the inhabitants of London or for export abroad. Lead ingots came from the Mendip Hills in Somerset and tin from Cornwall. Pewter vessels were made from a combination of the two metals. Purbeck marble from Dorset was used in buildings and for mortars, pestles and cosmetic palettes, while shale, from Kimmeridge in Dorset, was carved to make furniture, trays and bangles. Distinctive black jewellery and hair ornaments were made of jet from Whitby in Yorkshire. **7** All these goods contributed at various times to the rich cosmopolitan life of the city over nearly 400 years.

6

7 Part of a jet bracelet and 41 jet beads recovered from a late Roman burial at Spitalfields

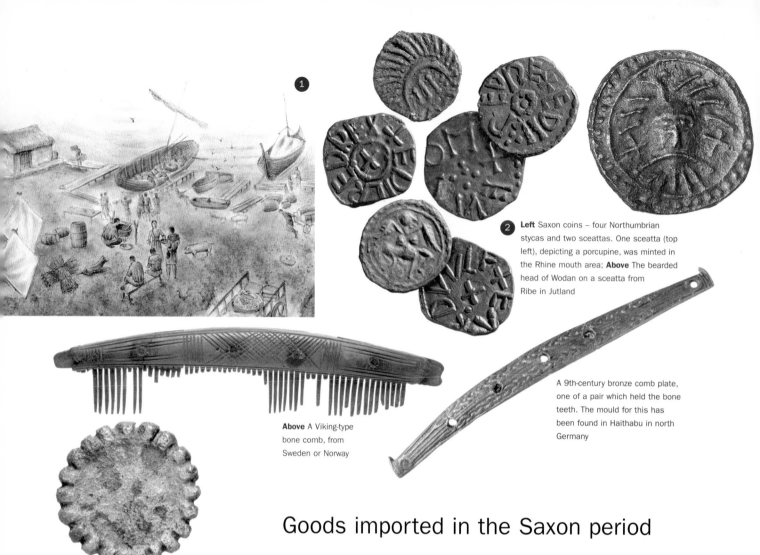

Left Saxon coins – four Northumbrian stycas and two sceattas. One sceatta (top left), depicting a porcupine, was minted in the Rhine mouth area; **Above** The bearded head of Wodan on a sceatta from Ribe in Jutland

A 9th-century bronze comb plate, one of a pair which held the bone teeth. The mould for this has been found in Haithabu in north Germany

Above A Viking-type bone comb, from Sweden or Norway

Above A German brooch – it probably originally held an enamelled design; **Below** A finely worked late 10th-century Germanic bronze mount found at the Guildhall. It may have been a decorative mount for a Bible since it appears to depict an Old Testament figure surrounded by vines

Goods imported in the Saxon period

From the seventh to ninth centuries the centre for London's trade was in the settlement of Lundenwic. At first transactions may have been carried out on the beach 1 or on board ship, but by about 680 Lundenwic was described as a port and must therefore have had docks. For most of the eighth century Lundenwic served as the port for the inland kingdom of Mercia. Commodities were exchanged with Hamwic (Southampton), Ipswich and York, and markets in northern France and the Low Countries, through which goods from the Meuse Valley, the Rhineland and other areas also passed. In the late ninth and tenth centuries a new market was created by Alfred at Queenhithe, within the recolonised walled city. There was some contact with the Rhineland and Denmark, but trade was now mainly regional. By about 1000, however, merchants from France and from towns in the Meuse Valley were again regularly visiting the city.

The main indicators of trade excavated by archaeologists for the seventh to the eleventh centuries are coins, pottery and items of stone. Apart from hoards, some 55 coins called sceattas, dating to the late seventh and eighth centuries, have been found in London. Most appear to be from London, Kent and Essex, but one is perhaps from Hamwic. One coin is certainly Frisian and another is a copy of a type originating in Ribe. 2 Continental coins are rare finds from the tenth and eleventh centuries, but include a few from the Low Countries.

Pottery was imported from other English regions and from the continent. Most of the pottery found in London dating from the eighth and ninth centuries originated in

Above Amber and stone hones from the Baltic; **Left** Late 8th-century bossed and stamped north French greyware from Belgium; **Below** A cowrie shell found at the Royal Opera House

Above top Badorf ware pot, produced at one of a number of centres near Cologne, Germany; **Above** A fragment from an Ipswich ware pitcher with a typical decoration of opposed gridded triangle stamps

Ipswich and northern France or the Low Countries. ❸ Other imported pottery includes Rhenish wares and a few types that probably derive from the Seine Valley. From about 900 to 1050 almost all London's pottery was imported from Oxfordshire, though from about 1000 wares from East Anglia (Thetford ware) and the Midlands (Stamford ware, St Neots ware) appear. At the same time pottery made in the valleys of the Seine, the Meuse and the Rhine also began to reach London. The English wares are mainly utilitarian while the imports comprise pitchers and amphorae that probably arrived in London as by-products of the wine trade.

Imported stone objects take the form of querns and hones (whetstones). ❹ Some are of Kentish stone, but most querns are of Niedermendig lava (from the Rhineland),

while a few rare hones were imported from Norway. Glass vessels and beads were imported from the continent (mainly the Rhineland), and possibly East Anglia, from the seventh to ninth centuries. And in the late ninth and tenth centuries items of metalwork from Denmark and Germany also began to reach London. The most exotic finds include cowrie shells ❺ that were placed in seventh-century graves, and fragments of tenth-century silk cloth, both from the east Mediterranean. Imported foodstuffs include fish from the North Sea, oysters from Essex and Suffolk, and lentils, grapes and figs. Other perishable goods were also imported, although these are less easy to find, including cloth and fur, raw materials for crafts such as metalworking or carpentry and wool for weaving.

Above A beautiful 10th-century pewter disc brooch. Parellels for this have been found at Lund in Sweden and at Mainz in Germany; **Below** A very rare lead seal from Byzantium, possibly 11th-century. The poorly registered Greek text shows that this was from the 'genikon', the office of financial administration in Constantinople

Above Quernstones imported as partially worked stock from the Eifel Mountains in Germany. Possibly damaged in transit, they were dumped at the dockside

Above Spanish 'cuerda seca' floor tile, decorated with Islamic-style motif and manufactured in Seville *c.* 1500; **Below** Decorated floor tiles from Buckinghamshire

Above This fragment of striped cloth made of very fine silk is a rare discovery in London. A luxury item, it was probably woven in Spain, where by royal decree such fabric was prohibited to all but those of highest rank; **Below** A fragment of cloth of silver – 98% pure silver twisted around a linen or hemp core and woven with silk. It probably came from an Islamic workshop in southern Spain in the 13th century

Goods imported into medieval London

In the early medieval period Queenhithe and Billingsgate were the main trading areas, but gradually the whole waterfront was developed. From the twelfth century until 1500, London's trade was dominated by the Hanse, a commercial and political league of Germanic towns, and most English commerce was channelled through the capital.

As always, London was both a centre of consumption and a point of redistribution for the rest of England. In addition to finished goods, a range of raw materials for crafts and the building industry were unloaded at its port. Caen stone from Normandy and Purbeck marble from Dorset were favoured for prestigious twelfth- and thirteenth-century buildings, while bricks from the Low Countries were used in the Tower of London in the late thirteenth century. Most floor tiles came from Buckinghamshire, but plain floor tiles

were also imported from the Netherlands. Scales, weights, seals and coins, all found in London, demonstrate commercial activity. Coins come from as far afield as Byzantium (Istanbul), with many from France, the Low Countries and Germany. Barrels and French and Rhenish pottery testify to the wine trade, and seeds from exotic foodstuffs include spices, figs and grapes.

London's own wool industry was surpassed by imports of finished cloth during the late fourteenth century to supply the church and the nobility. The range of fabrics found in London is far greater than in other north European towns, and includes fragments from two high-quality patterned silk vestments, probably from Islamic Spain, and late fourteenth-century Italian silk and satin damask. A thirteenth-century Chinese twill damask reflects the reopening of trade routes to the Far East. Lead cloth seals were introduced in the fourteenth century

Right Coral was imported from the Mediterranean and has been used to form the decorative heads of these dress pins

Below This exquisite glass beaker stands about 10 cm high and is decorated with white enamel dots and gold leaf which has been etched with lettering and alternating bands of laurel and oak leaves. Found in a cesspit in Great Tower Street in the City, it was probably made in Venice in about 1500

Above 15th-century lustreware from Valencia; **Above right** A Montelupo Cavalier dish from Italy, dated to the period 1575–1620; **Right** A rare imported Italian tin-glazed jug from a 16th-century cesspit in the City. The jug, which was probably manufactured in Faenza, is hand-decorated with the three hills of Calvary, the cross with the crown of thorns and other symbols of the Passion

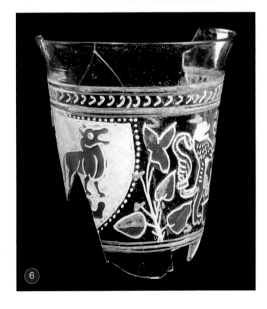

as a means of indicating the source, quality and quantity of textiles. London has the richest collection of such seals in England, with several thousand examples. Seals from at least fourteen different English counties have been identified (mainly Essex and Norfolk), with a number from the continent, particularly Germany (especially Augsburg).

Surrounding counties, notably Surrey and Hertfordshire, supplied pottery for domestic use. In the twelfth to fourteenth centuries most continental pottery originated in France, with examples of German pottery only appearing in the area of the German Guildhall. Between 1250 and 1350 imported pottery forms a very minor element of most assemblages in London, but after that period Rhenish stoneware was imported in larger quantities. Both this and Saintonge ware (from Bordeaux) ③ probably reached London as by-products

of the wine trade. Spanish ④ and Italian pottery ⑤ are less frequent finds, but appear in contexts dating from the 1270s and increase in the later fourteenth century when trade with Spain and the Mediterranean flourished and the fashion for pieces for display caught on.

Imported metalwork would have been limited to the upper classes, guilds and other institutions. Imported glass vessels are very rare but include fragments of fourteenth-century drinking cups and goblets from Italy and southern France, and one piece that may be from the Near East. Of particular interest are a number of thirteenth- or fourteenth-century Italian 'Aldrevandini' enamelled beakers. ⑥ Fragments from up to eight examples were found in one cesspit, together with local pottery and metalworking debris, suggesting they were discarded from a jeweller's shop.

Above Part of a 16th-century Raeren stoneware jug, depicting Themis, the goddess of order and justice; **Below** Pallisy-type ware from the Loire Valley in France, found in a stone-lined well in the Fleet valley

2 Late 17th-century Westerwald tankards from the Rhineland, found thrown into a household rubbish pit on the site at Poultry

Above A Dutch wall tile of late 17th-century date, with a mounted military figure; **Right** A complete pale-green glass flask from Germany. Made in the early 16th century, it would have held perfume, medicine or possibly holy water. It was found in a 17th-century cesspit in St John Street

Goods imported into post-medieval London

An early eighteenth-century guidebook described London as 'the chiefest Emporium or Town of Trade in the World', whose contacts stretched across the globe. Most of the perishable trade goods that entered London have long since disappeared, but the pottery that frequently accompanied them is recovered by archaeologists in huge quantities.

German stonewares from the Rhineland are the most widespread of all imported wares, with the well-known Bartmann jugs or 'Bellarmines' 1 from Cologne and Frechen arriving in vast numbers during the sixteenth and seventeenth centuries. Used to decant wine from casks, these vessels, with their often grotesque bearded face-masks, must have been a very familiar sight in inns and taverns. Rather more elaborate, Westerwald stoneware, also from the Rhineland, is decorated in cobalt blue and sometimes manganese purple. 2

During the sixteenth and early seventeenth centuries influences from the Low Countries were increasingly evident in London, as large numbers of religious refugees settled in the capital. One such group were the Huguenots, French Protestants who were subjected to religious persecution from 1685.

Red earthenwares arrived both as trade goods and along with merchants, sailors and settlers – including no doubt potters who brought their own techniques and styles with them. These influences had a pronounced effect on London's ceramic industries, and it was Flemish potters who introduced the technique of tin-glazing in the 1570s. The English tin-glazed industry flourished in the seventeenth and eighteenth centuries at the expense of Dutch decorated wares, which are found only rarely in London, but include a dish depicting the spies sent by Moses into Canaan. Interestingly, unlike in other cities such as Canterbury, there is little evidence of the Huguenots in the pottery found in their houses. Perhaps their origin was reflected more in the food they ate than the pottery they used.

Left An extremely rare 17th-century Persian porcelain bowl, from a cesspit on the Lloyds Register site in the City; **Below** 16th-century German counters found at the Rose theatre

A group of Chinese porcelain teabowls, early 18th century

Left A rare glass cup; **Below** 17th-century bowling balls of lignum vitae wood, from South America

Flasks and jugs associated with the wine trade came from Normandy and south-west France. A more unusual piece from this area is an elaborately decorated, and extremely rare, late sixteenth-century pedestal bowl, or tazza, depicting a scene with Minerva, Cupid and six other figures.

Pottery from Spain and Portugal arrived both as containers for goods such as olive oil, honey and wine, and occasionally as fine, decorative tablewares valued as display items. A colourful mid seventeenth-century dish from Portugal depicts a leaping hare ❸ and was inspired by Chinese export wares. Imports from Italy are often very decorative, and would have been highly displayable, luxury items, such as a tazza made in Urbino, Deruta or Faenza. It is finely painted with birds, snails and assorted 'grotesques' inspired by wall paintings in the underground caverns of Nero's palace in Rome.

One of the most unusual groups of imported pottery came from Kirman, in central southern Iran. It includes a seventeenth-century bowl and plate decorated with Chinese-inspired designs. So far unique in London, they probably represent travellers' souvenirs.

Imported pottery declines in the late seventeenth century as a result no doubt of disruptions to production caused by the Thirty Years War. Chinese porcelain, however, continued to exert a powerful influence on English taste, style and design, entering London in massive quantities in the cargoes of the East India Company right up to the end of the eighteenth century. ❹ Initially a rare and precious commodity only accessible to the wealthy (Queen Elizabeth I had a collection), by the mid-eighteenth century blue and white export porcelain was widely available and increasingly popular as the craze for hot drinks, with which it went hand-in-hand, swept the country.

London's houses

Timber houses

London's earliest dwellings were made from wood and earth.

Whatever simple shelters were constructed by the earliest groups of hunter gatherers during the Upper Palaeolithic (*c.* 21,000–8000 BC) and Mesolithic (*c.* 8000–4000 BC) periods, they have left no trace in the area that is now Greater London. Being nomadic, these people did not build long-term, permanent houses, which makes the task of finding them particularly difficult for archaeologists. The earliest excavated huts or houses date from the Neolithic period (*c.* 4000–2000 BC), when people gradually settled down and adopted an agricultural lifestyle. During the following Bronze and Iron Ages (*c.* 2000 BC–AD 43), the most common form of structure in use was the

roundhouse. **1** Walls were constructed of large posts set into the ground at intervals to form circles, ranging from 3 to 12 m in diameter. The gaps in between the posts were probably filled in with wattle and daub – interwoven branches and twigs covered with mud. Pieces of burnt daub survive, preserving the impressions of the wattle lattice. Evidence from Iron Age sites in east and west London shows that shallow ditches encircled the huts to catch rainwater running off the roof, thus keeping the area around the building dry. The entrances to the Iron Age huts are clearly marked by gaps in these 'eaves drip gullies', and holes for additional posts

indicate the presence of porches to protect doorways from the rain.

The native tradition of building these roundhouses continued during the early years of the Roman occupation, and examples have been found not only on rural farmsteads but also on the margins of Roman Londinium. Several first-century circular 'British' buildings were excavated in the north-west corner of the City, right at the edge of the settlement. These houses were replaced when a new Roman road and rectilinear 'Roman' buildings were built as the town expanded. **2** This change from a circular to a rectangular form is a common,

Right An almost complete door from a Roman house was found at Poultry, reused as an area of flooring in a 1st-century building

although not universal, difference between 'British' and 'Roman' houses. Though different in shape, the new houses were often still built of timber, reflecting both the frontier character of the Roman town as well as the availability of oak and lack of local building stone. ❸ In a matter of about 70 years the number of inhabitants in Londinium had grown to 20,000 or more as the city became home to a cosmopolitan population from Britain and the continent, made up of prosperous citizens, freedmen, slaves and the poor – a mix that was reflected in the housing stock.

The design, construction and function of individual buildings have been identified at many archaeological sites, in particular around the main east–west street where it crossed the Walbrook stream. Here, the homes and businesses of first-century Londoners were located in single-storey, timber-framed buildings with walls of earth, mudbrick, ❹ or lath and plaster ❺ set on earth or timber sills. Exteriors were whitewashed or weather-boarded, and roofs thatched, boarded or shingled. Farm animals and noxious industries were located side-by-side with living quarters. Many fairly ordinary residential buildings included shops, workshops and storerooms, with small-scale manufacturing taking place in yards. Roadside houses were set very close together, with narrow frontages measuring just 5 to 6 m but extending 15 to 30 m away from the road. Corridors and alleys ❻ led to back rooms and yards. More substantial late first-century timber-framed buildings nearby measured up to 20 by 50 m and included up to twelve rooms, perhaps used by a number of families.

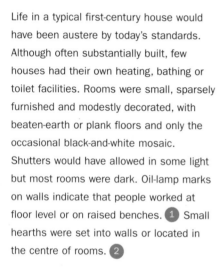

Above The chains and hook allowed this superbly preserved 1st-century bronze oil-lamp to be carried about and fixed from existing fittings or from wall studs in the house; **Left** Two late 4th-century Roman hearths

Above An 11th-century wattle-and-post building beside a cobbled pathway (the concrete column is a modern pile); **Above right** Grooved posts set 2 or 3 m apart allowed horizontal planks to slot in to form timber walls. This example comes from a building at the Guildhall site which, despite repeated partial destruction by fire, appears to have been lived in from around 1040 through into the 12th century

Below A reconstruction of one of the 11th-century buildings found on the Guildhall site. Constructed of wattlework panels set between large upright timber posts and rendered with a mixture of animal dung and straw, it had a floor of beaten earth

Life in a typical first-century house would have been austere by today's standards. Although often substantially built, few houses had their own heating, bathing or toilet facilities. Rooms were small, sparsely furnished and modestly decorated, with beaten-earth or plank floors and only the occasional black-and-white mosaic. Shutters would have allowed in some light but most rooms were dark. Oil-lamp marks on walls indicate that people worked at floor level or on raised benches. ① Small hearths were set into walls or located in the centre of rooms. ②

A prominent room in a Roman Londoner's home might be used for a variety of family and business functions during the day, including religious worship, but become a dining room in the evening and a bedroom at night. The average life-span of London's timber buildings was short – 20 to 40 years – in part due to frequent fires, subsidence and the ravages of weather. None the less, precisely maintained boundaries reveal that care was taken over property ownership and security even for the humblest buildings, even after widespread fires necessitated total rebuilding.

Houses in the Saxon period were generally built from timber, wattle and daub. Mostly relatively small, they too would have been used for crafts, shops and keeping animals, as well as for housing. Timber posts were usually set into the ground in the corners and sometimes along the walls with panels of wattle and daub fixed between. ③

Two house types predominate in this period. The first, generally single-storey, was built at ground level, with partitions separating the various rooms. Floors would have been of simple materials, such as clay or brickearth covered in rushes. Many such buildings have been found in Lundenwic. A particularly good example from the very late Saxon period, around the middle of the eleventh century, fronted on to Lawrence Lane near the Guildhall in the City. ④ It measured about 10 m long by 5 m wide and had an entrance passage, a kitchen

Above This Saxon oven at Mortlake was attached to a building with characteristic sunken floors; **Left** Houses in Saxon Lundenwic, based on archaeological evidence from the Royal Opera House

Below The reuse of timber from boats and buildings has led to some remarkable survivals. At a site just east of Queenhithe three structural timbers, originally part of a substantial aisled building, appeared as part of a 10th-century revetment; **Right** The excavated timbers; **Below left** Drawing of an aisled building showing the timbers in place

Above The remains of Saxon sunken houses at Hammersmith and Heathrow

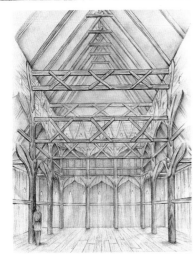

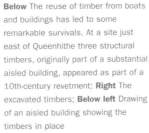

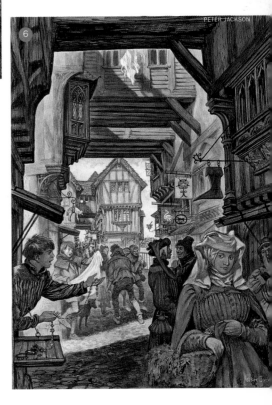

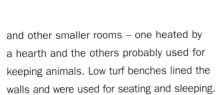

and other smaller rooms – one heated by a hearth and the others probably used for keeping animals. Low turf benches lined the walls and were used for seating and sleeping.

The other classic type of Saxon house was the 'sunken-floored building'. ⑤ As its name suggests, the floor, usually of beaten earth, was sunk below ground level by perhaps as much as 1 m. Posts supported the roof at the corners, and the walls were often made from planks. These houses were rarely large, often being only 3 or 4 m square. Examples have been found in smaller settlements and in the reoccupied walled City, but not in Lundenwic itself.

Most of London's medieval housing was also built of timber and was thus almost entirely destroyed by the Great Fire of 1666. Buildings were often jettied – that is extended out over the street at upper levels at the front to create more space inside the house. ⑥ Houses on narrow alleys were consequently very close to each other at first-floor level. Improved timber building techniques allowed for two- or three-storey houses and these were often divided both horizontally and vertically, with shops or workshops on the ground floor and living quarters on other floors. Sometimes several families occupied one house.

Above left The walls and part of a mosaic floor from a late Roman building at 1 Poultry; **Above right** Part of a Roman Tuscan order column, with traces of paint just visible between the moulded bands on the capital. Although not *in situ*, it was found on the site of a high-status Roman building in the city and may have formed part of an external portico facing the river

Above top A reconstructed room from a Roman house in the Museum of London; **Above** The plaster on the pointing between the stone blocks in this Roman wall has been painted with thin red lines, resulting in a curious combination of rustication and ashlar effect

Stone houses

Stone buildings leave better evidence and were often owned by the wealthier members of society.

Right A 2nd-century stone building found under Borough High Street; **Below right** Collapsed and discarded Roman wall plaster is uncovered on a site in the city; **Below** The richly coloured head of Bacchus depicted on wall plaster

By the middle of the second century AD Roman Londinium's inhabitants began to build larger stone houses that were set back from the road. ❶ These townhouses – some with rooms opening onto a corridor with wings at either end – created a more obvious display of wealth and status than timber buildings, ❷ but little is known about the occupants. We do not even know if they owned or rented the properties. Rooms within these buildings perhaps had more clearly defined functions than in the earlier, humbler timber structures. The continental model for a wealthy Roman townhouse normally consisted of a central courtyard with the other rooms opening off it, but only a few of the largest buildings in London followed this pattern. One such is the late Roman building excavated at Plantation Place, just to the south of the forum, which had its own tower and cellar

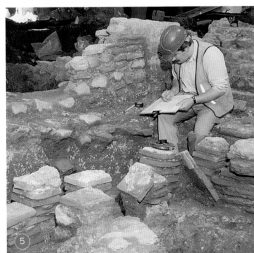

Above Decorated flue-tiles were used to carry the warmed air from the hypocaust up the surrounding walls; **Below** A Roman ceramic chimney

Below *In situ* wall plaster

Above A mosaic floor from 1 Poultry; **Above right** A mosaic floor in Southwark. Often these mosaics had a decorated pattern in the centre surrounded by a border and a plain area beyond, an effect similar to a rug in a modern room

strong-room – a clear sign that the owner was wealthy and had goods that needed safekeeping.

Timber buildings are still found in third- and fourth-century London, but, as archaeologists have discovered on sites in the centre of the Roman town, in the third century these were often enhanced by stone additions. ③ Rich merchants desiring better reception areas and living quarters behind long-established businesses perhaps retained their original timber houses but added to them in the more impressive and up-to-date stone construction.

Wealthy citizens may have maintained a villa in the country in addition to their house in town. A considerable number of well-appointed stone buildings have been excavated in the area near the Walbrook,

in the heart of the Roman city, including some with underfloor heating and mosaic paving. ④ One building contained an apsidal room and a magnificent mosaic known as the Bucklersbury Pavement, now displayed in the Museum of London. Underfloor heating systems, known as hypocausts, ⑤ are one of the clearest indications of wealthier inhabitants. The mixture of detached stone buildings, empty plots of ground, gardens and surviving timber buildings gave the late Roman town a very different look and feel from its frontier ancestor, though it retained the same untidy character, with yards containing refuse and manure heaps overgrown with weeds. All of this suggests a much smaller population in London in the third and fourth centuries, although some of the inhabitants seem to have been much wealthier than their predecessors.

Private houses may have been the last refuge for Romanised residents, even after many of London's public buildings, such as the forum and the amphitheatre, had fallen into decay. Evocative evidence of London's final decline at the end of the fourth century can be seen in the neat removal of mosaic panels from floors in some of these fine stone buildings, and their replacement with rudimentary patches of roofing tile. ⑥ The mosaics were apparently salvaged but the buildings continued to be occupied for a short time – either by owners fallen on hard times or squatters.

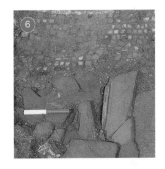

Above Part of a red and gold capital, dating to about 1400; **Left** A carved animal's head, possibly from a doorway, found at Spitalfields; **Right bottom** A floor tile found at Bishopsgate

Above The foundations of this 12th-century warehouse at Queenhithe, possibly built as part of the revitalisation of the dock by Queen Matilda, were built on timber rafts

After the decline of the Roman Empire, stone was not used again by Londoners for their ordinary residences until the twelfth century. And in many cases it was even then used only for foundations, as it prevented the timber-frames of the houses rotting so quickly in the ground and provided greater support for multi-storey buildings. ① People also began to build stone cellars, probably for storing foodstuffs, with fine examples excavated near the dockside in the City and also within monastic precincts such as at St Mary Spital ② and St Mary Clerkenwell in the immediate London hinterland. Kentish ragstone was the commonest stone used, with greensand from Surrey preferred for any carved stonework and chalk for foundations. Flint was also a popular durable exterior material.

Houses within monasteries were often lived in by artisans or lay residents. Artisans' dwellings tended to reflect their more modest needs and wealth – perhaps two rooms for a workshop and living area and a yard which was often used to dispose of the remains of whatever trade they practised. In fact such waste often reveals the nature of their trade. At Milk Street in the City, crucibles containing silver and practice designs for brooches suggest metalworkers were living and working there. The lay residents in monastic precincts might be much wealthier and would sometimes have multi-roomed structures, with separate areas for eating, sleeping and cooking arranged around a yard.

Heating was usually provided by a hearth or fireplace – typically in the middle of the

room in the early periods and against the walls later on. Hearths were often made of roofing tiles laid on edge and set in clay. ③ Similar hearths were used for cooking, though evidence of spits for roasting meat is also found, and larger structures had ovens. Floors were frequently simply of beaten earth or mortar, strewn with straw. A tile grate by the door was used to scrape mud from boots and shoes, but this did not prevent the floors frequently wearing away and needing replacement. Only the wealthiest could afford a tiled floor.

Right A chalk cellar associated with buildings at the Guildhall

Above A medieval stone corbel in the form of a human head

An impressive vaulted cellar of chalk and flint, perhaps belonging to a merchant's house, on the road leading to Kingston Bridge. Steps led down into it from the street

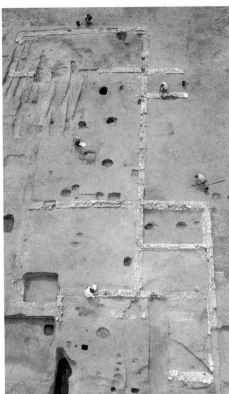

Above Foundations of the manor house at Low Hall in east London; **Left** The vaulted undercroft at Syon House, Brentford, built on the site of Syon Abbey after the Dissolution in 1539

Merchants usually wanted their houses to reflect and display their wealth, ④ and they would buy up many smaller properties in the city and create a larger mansion on the site, often with ranges around a courtyard. Many manor houses outside the central core of London were moated, both for defence and to serve as fishponds. Edward II had a house known as the Rosary on the south side of the river, opposite the Tower of London, which was later bought and rebuilt by Sir John Fastolf, made famous by Shakespeare as Falstaff. Another manor, somewhat further out in what was then open countryside, was at Low Hall, ⑤ now in Walthamstow, which was once owned by Warwick the Kingmaker who in 1461 helped depose Henry VI and bring Edward IV to the throne. The earliest building on the site had stone foundations, probably for a timber frame. It comprised a hall and solar (upper chamber) with a service range at one end. A moat surrounded the whole complex, crossed by a wooden bridge dating to 1344 ⑥ which archaeologists found still partially surviving. The house was subsequently extended by the addition of a second wing. A collection of floor tiles made at Penn in Buckinghamshire give a picture of the decoration inside the house.

Brick walls and floors of a cellared house at Spitalfields, dating from about 1600. The niche may have been for candles

Above The kitchen in the east wing at Sutton House, showing the original 16th-century fireplace blocked by 18th-century brickwork; **Below** The floor of this 16th-century building at Spitalfields was made from reused medieval tiles

Brick houses

One of today's most familiar building materials – brick – became popular in the 16th century.

The 17th-century brick floor in a tenement on 'Bull Court' in Southwark

From the sixteenth century on, the most significant change in the outward appearance of housing was the increasing use of brick. Houses from this period add another dimension to archaeology, because many are still standing, and recording them is an important element in our understanding of how people lived in the past.

Wealthy merchants and members of the aristocracy were keen to appear fashionable by decorating their houses in the new Jacobean style using brick and terracotta (ornamental pottery) and by having larger windows. Structures were often thus a mixture of old and new, but some areas offered fresh opportunities for building from scratch. In particular, the former

lands of the monastic houses dissolved by Henry VIII became the sites of aristocratic mansions. The Dukes of Newcastle had a house at St Mary Clerkenwell and the Dukes of Norfolk at the Charterhouse – before the Duke was executed at the behest of Elizabeth I for treason. More modest but still substantial brick houses have been excavated by archaeologists at Spitalfields, ① including multi-roomed houses with brick floors, cesspits and chimney stacks.

Other houses of the nobility were built further out of London, such as Sutton House in Hackney, ② originally built in the 1530s and owned by Thomas Sutton. The original form and layout of his house

Left One of the designs of elaborate 16th-century moulded terracotta bricks made to decorate a post-Dissolution house on the site of the former Priory of St John Clerkenwell

Above One of the cramped post-medieval tenements near the waterfront yielded nearly 2000 clay tobacco pipe fragments and evidence of a possibly illegal pre-Fire pipe kiln; **Below** The timber roofs of late 17th-century brick buildings on Middle Temple Lane

Early 17th-century brick-built cellars and cesspits in Islington

were ascertained by excavation. Built around a courtyard, it had four storeys, including a cellar. The line of the original rear walls of the house, which were demolished when the house was extended, was also found. Sutton founded the Charterhouse in the seventeenth century as both a school and a hospital for aged men. Buildings found on the west side of the precinct which may once have been the monastic barns of the old priory perhaps served to house the men. As was common at this time, earth floors were replaced in brick.

Remains of buildings preserved beneath the destruction levels of the Great Fire fill in some of the details of the fine houses that once stood in the City. Near London Bridge was Lombards Place, an imposing merchant's house dating from at least the fifteenth century. ③ Its late medieval cellars had brick floors, wooden staircases and new brick fireplaces and chimney stacks added – a sign of the increasing

comfort in houses of the age. Ceramic pots were found in the floors, a common feature to aid drainage. ④

The huge expansion in London's population led to the creation of new suburbs around the city. To the east, fine four- and five-storey brick terrace houses were built in Spitalfields from the 1660s through to the middle of the eighteenth century. Huguenot Protestants, fleeing Catholic repression in France, settled in the area and set up a major weaving industry. Many of the cellars of these houses have been excavated. Their back gardens have been found to contain a well for water and a cesspit for disposing of waste, often side-by-side – not a recipe for good health. Some of their cesspits contain entire clearances of a household's ceramics, a vivid illustration of the eviction of tenants in the nineteenth century when the silk-weaving industry collapsed.

Right Reconstruction of the palace at Westminster; Below Medieval tiles from houses in Westminster

Parliament was first called by the King in the 13th century. It has always resided at Westminster and the Houses of Parliament were built after the old palace burnt to the ground in 1834

Palaces

The Greater London area contains many of England's most important and historic royal palaces.

The principal residence of the Kings of England in the medieval period lay at Westminster, 1 and antiquarians have long been interested in this site, recording some buildings before their demolition and others that still stand. Archaeologists have also seized opportunities to excavate there whenever they arise. A palace certainly stood here, next to the Abbey, by the reign of Edward the Confessor (1042–65), if not before. The early medieval kings were itinerant, moving around the country from palace to palace or staying at courtiers' houses, but by the reign of Henry III in the thirteenth century, the main permanent royal residence was firmly established at Westminster. 2

The royal palace was situated on a defensible island at the junction of the River Tyburn with the Thames. It probably originally consisted of a simple hall and chambers for the king, but in the 1090s William II built an enormous new hall alongside the river, which still stands today. It was much altered in 1399 when Richard III had towers and a magnificent single-span timber roof added. Coronations and major ceremonial events were held here, and it was also the home of the law courts until the 1880s. Eventually the palace comprised four major courtyards – the outer one was a public space full of taverns and shops. One tavern next to the main gatehouse had a cesspit in which were found wooden plates and pieces of barrel. Next to the public court was the yard where the main offices of government were located, including the Exchequer (treasury) which was excavated in the 1880s. The wall dividing the yard from the outer ward has also been found. The inner court was the residential part of the palace. Here were the King's and Queen's apartments, the royal chapel of St Stephen's, the King's jewel tower and rooms for courtiers and royal favourites. Many of these buildings were recorded before their destruction in the 1830s and, more recently, archaeologists have found the foundations of the chapel and excavated the moat of the jewel tower. The major apartments were at first-floor level: the King's chamber (known as the Painted Chamber) and St Stephen's Chapel (the king's own chapel) were considered wonders of the age by writers from all over Europe.

There were other royal residences in London during the medieval period, although they were used more rarely. The Tower of London 3 was sometimes used

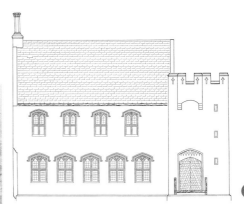

as a residence, and Edward III built himself a moated manor house down by the river in Rotherhithe 4 consisting of a rectangular enclosure filled with ranges of buildings and surrounded by a moat.

Henry VII rebuilt an earlier royal palace on the Thames at Richmond, perhaps as a calm retreat away from the crowded, busy centre of the metropolis. It became his favourite residence and he died there in 1509. Part of the brick gatehouse still survives and archaeologists have found some of the brick ranges within the inner enclosure. 5

London's other major royal palace was at Whitehall. This vast complex was the principal residence of the English monarchs and the seat of government throughout the sixteenth and seventeenth centuries. Like Westminster, it was destroyed by fire. The only major surviving building is Inigo Jones' Banqueting House, 6 although redevelopment of the Treasury in the 1960s uncovered tennis courts, cockpits and many other areas for games and pastimes.

Left Part of the moated manor house known as Fastolf's Place, in Southwark. Part of an elaborate early 15th-century oak-panelled door from the house was discovered in the moat

Above The interior of the Old Hall of the Bishop of Chichester's Inn on Chancery Lane

London contains other grand houses that have often been described as palaces, although they were usually the residences of bishops, archbishops and wealthy nobles. Most of these people would have owned various residences around the country, but all required a house close to the seat of royal and political power in London.

Many of the bishops' London houses were situated along the road between the City and Westminster – Fleet Street and the Strand – giving them access to both the political and financial centres of power. ① The Bishops of Norwich, Lincoln and Durham had their houses here, and John of Gaunt, son of Edward III, had a fine house where the Savoy Hotel now stands. ② Archaeologists have as yet barely touched

on this very interesting aspect of London's archaeology and it remains one of our most important areas of research in the future.

A number of ecclesiastical residences have been excavated, however, including that belonging to the Archbishop of York close to Westminster. Excavations in the 1930s found the great hall, private hall and chapel linked by a cloister, as well as a long stretch of stone river wall fronting the Thames. The Bishop of Ely, meanwhile, had his London residence off Newgate, near where Holborn Circus is now. Walls of some of the buildings have been excavated, and the chapel, dedicated to St Etheldreda, still stands. ③

A gilded stone, probably from the Yellow Room in the east wing at Somerset House, used by the Queen's Maids of Honour. The palace was extensively and lavishly refurbished by Queen Anne of Denmark, the wife of James I, in the 17th century

Right A gold ring set with a garnet, probably 14th century in date, found in the backfill to the Great Drain of Winchester Palace

4

5

Above Moulded stones from the demolition of Somerset House in 1775; Below A gilded stucco mask from the Duke of Somerset's palace on the Strand gives an indication of the high quality of Renaissance-style architecture which the building must have embodied

Two other important ecclesiastical mansions that have been excavated are the Archbishop of Canterbury's palace at Lambeth, 4 where the tiled floor of the chapel has been revealed, and the Bishop of Winchester's house in Southwark. Here, large-scale excavations over many years have uncovered a vast range of buildings to accommodate a huge retinue associated with one of England's most important prelates. Founded in the middle of the twelfth century, the palace lay in the Bishop of Winchester's diocese and had its own chapel and a great hall with a kitchen range attached. In the thirteenth century the great hall was divided into two by a large wall with a fine rose window that still survives. 5 Important ceremonies and massive feasts would have taken place in the great hall, while the

bishop would have had smaller rooms set aside for his personal use. Decoration within the palace would have been of the highest quality, with coloured and patterned tiles on the floors and hangings or paintings embellishing the walls. Later additions included ranges of buildings around courtyards for squires and knights. The palace also had its own dock, vital for travelling around the region at this time.

Of the great baronial mansions, one that was the home of Protector Somerset, regent of England during the childhood reign of Edward VI in the mid sixteenth century, has been excavated on the banks of the Thames. The house was substantially rebuilt in the nineteenth century, but remains of the brick walls of the original Tudor house

still stand to first-floor level beneath the courtyard. Somerset House is known to have been built from many of the stones robbed from monastic houses when they were demolished in the 1530s and 1540s. 6

6

London at home

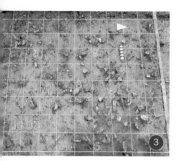

Above left Excavations at Uxbridge revealed scatters of bones of reindeer and wild horse, together with the flint tools used to butcher them

Above Amphorae were made in a variety of shapes and sizes according to use; Right Roman copper alloy figure of Bacchus, the god of wine, holding baskets overflowing with grapes

Diet in London

Environmental archaeology can tell us a great deal about people's diet and how it changed over the centuries, providing fascinating insights into the lives of Londoners and greatly enhancing our understanding of our past.

Left Sieving can catch tiny pieces of evidence that may otherwise escape notice; Right Fine fish bones retrieved by sieving; Below right Large quantites of charred cereal grain suggest that the Roman building destroyed by fire in which they were found may have been a bakery

Details of food production, trade and even the status of individuals are all revealed by the animal bones ❶ and other refuse discarded in pits and grain and seeds ❷ which survive because they have been either charred or waterlogged.

One of our earliest glimpses into the population's diet comes from an upper Palaeolithic hunting camp dating to around 10,000 BC excavated in west London. ❸ Remains showed that its inhabitants were eating animals such as red deer, reindeer, roe deer, teal, fox and beaver. The climate was certainly cooler at this period, which may account for the emphasis on a meat-rich diet. With the onset of farming during the Neolithic period, people began to eat more cereals, such as barley, smelt and emmer, as well as meat, including beef, mutton, deer ❹ and aurochs (an extinct type of ox).

In the Roman period the huge increase in trade and the range of foodstuffs imported

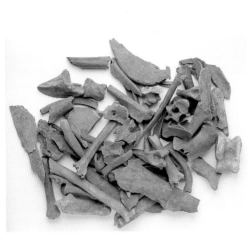

A very large quantity of butchered cattle bones was recovered from a Roman building in Southwark. They were found in two distinct groups, one comprising the 'choicest cuts' and the other containing the skull and lower legs which would have yielded poorer meat. The building was very likely a butcher's shop, where animals were (probably) killed and jointed, and the meat sold

Above The bones of four-horned sheep suggest that there was a Scandinavian presence in the City. This type of sheep is today represented in Britain by the Jacob, Manx Loughtan and Black Hebridean breeds, all of which are considered to have derived from sheep brought to this country by the Vikings

Right Discarded oyster shells dumped against the side of a late Roman wall. Oysters were part of Londoners' staple diet for centuries; plentiful and cheap, they were regarded very differently from the luxury item of today

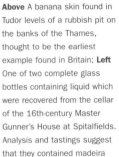

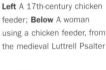

Above A banana skin found in Tudor levels of a rubbish pit on the banks of the Thames, thought to be the earliest example found in Britain; **Left** One of two complete glass bottles containing liquid which were recovered from the cellar of the 16th-century Master Gunner's House at Spitalfields. Analysis and tastings suggest that they contained madeira
Left A 17th-century chicken feeder; **Below** A woman using a chicken feeder, from the medieval Luttrell Psalter

brought great changes to Londoners' diet. Cereal agriculture was still important but a much greater diversity of food was now available. People ate more chicken and pig, fish was plentiful and oysters seem to have been a staple. Fruit remains are much more common at this time, with fig and grape seeds regularly found at sites all over the city. Pear, apple, cherry and plum are rather less frequent finds, and olives are relatively rare. Pulses such as lentils and peas were also eaten, although these do not survive in the archaeological record so well. Wine was imported in large quantities – it was carried and stored in large clay vessels known as amphorae. **5** There is even evidence of garum, a piquant fish sauce: this was imported in amphorae which carry impressed stamps showing they originated in Antibes, on the south coast of France.

In the Saxon period Londoners were restricted to a less exotic and varied diet. Meat consisted mainly of beef and mutton, and more rarely chicken, pig and fish. **6** Cereals seem to have formed the staple part of the diet, with fruit and vegetables much less common, although peas and horse beans (similar to broad beans) were eaten. No doubt this change in diet was a result of decreased trade and the decline in infrastructure of farms and transportation.

With the re-emergence of London as a trading and commercial centre during the medieval period, the diet of its inhabitants was once again similar to that of Roman Londoners, although imported foodstuffs were still perhaps less common. Meat and fish and shellfish – marine **7** and freshwater – were fundamental elements of the diet, but cereals, some fruit and vegetables and dairy products were also eaten. London's food supply network became increasingly sophisticated as it developed to cater for an expanding population. Fowl and pigs might be reared locally by individuals, while beef and mutton were brought on the hoof to London from far afield for slaughter. Cereals were also transported greater distances, but perishable foodstuffs such as dairy products and fruit were produced close to the city.

From the seventeenth century onwards the rapid growth of exploration all around the globe brought a huge array of imported foodstuffs to add to the diet Londoners. These included such exotic goods as citrus fruits, dates and spices from the Americas – foods that are regarded as commonplace today. **8**

Left A Delftware plate of the 1720s made in Lambeth, with an inscription in Hebrew – 'chlav' ('milk'). The plate would have been part of two separate sets for meals; Jewish dietary laws require dairy and meat produce to be kept apart

Above A 1st-century samian drinking cup, from southern Gaul; **Right** A box-wood scoop with a handle in the form of an exotic head with negroid features

Above View across two rooms of an early 2nd-century Roman building. The room in the foreground, separated from other parts of the building by brickearth walls, was probably a kitchen, containing pottery which was broken and scattered across the floor when the building was destroyed by a fire

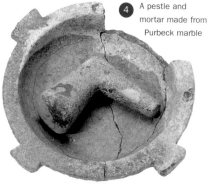

A pestle and mortar made from Purbeck marble

In the kitchen

A wide range of equipment and vessels survives from London's kitchens.

A typical Roman kitchen of the first century AD might contain a simple hearth, often at floor level though sometimes it was raised, with space beneath the platform for storing fuel. A copper alloy pot standing on a gridiron over the hearth was used for cooking, and an array of foodstuffs and metal utensils would hang from hooks around the room. **1** Although expensive, metal may have been preferred to pottery for cooking as it was more durable and easier to clean. **2** Few houses had a supply of piped water so it had to be carried from wells or cisterns and stored in wooden buckets.

Vessels for storage and serving were of imported and local pottery, while mould-blown glass bottles **3** were used for transporting and storing liquids and loose foodstuffs, such as olives. Ingredients were pounded using a pestle and mortar. **4** Ceramic mortaria, the Roman equivalent of the food processor, were gritted on the inside surface to aid the mixing and grinding of herbs and other foods and were often stamped on the rim with the name of the potter. Bread was cooked in the local baker's oven, **5** but the dough was first mixed and kneaded in wooden troughs, which retained heat during the rising process.

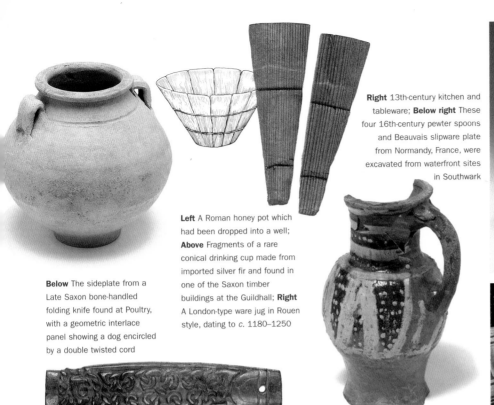

Right 13th-century kitchen and tableware; **Below right** These four 16th-century pewter spoons and Beauvais slipware plate from Normandy, France, were excavated from waterfront sites in Southwark

Left A Roman honey pot which had been dropped into a well; **Above** Fragments of a rare conical drinking cup made from imported silver fir and found in one of the Saxon timber buildings at the Guildhall; **Right** A London-type ware jug in Rouen style, dating to *c.* 1180–1250

Below The sideplate from a Late Saxon bone-handled folding knife found at Poultry, with a geometric interlace panel showing a dog encircled by a double twisted cord

Right Mid 19th-century pearlware plate decorated with a cockroach

In the medieval period, if the household could afford it, cooking vessels were made of metal rather than pottery and usually consisted of a sheet or cast copper alloy cauldron for making stews. Sheet vessels were the cheaper of the metal options because they could be more easily produced – by hammering rather than casting (which required a special furnace and a higher level of skill) – as well as using far less metal to make. Sheeting was vulnerable to splitting, while cast items were prone to shattering; broken-off feet or replacements that had become detached are the most common finds from copper alloy cooking vessels. Dripping pans placed under spit roasts seem only exceptionally to have been of metal. A pewter serving vessel for wine or beer had generally taken the place of a decorative earthenware jug by the end of the medieval period, though even fragments are unusual finds because this metal could be recycled. In the sixteenth century pewter serving plates had become common. ❻ In some houses,

other food-preparation vessels such as chafing dishes (again available in both metal and ceramic) were in regular use. Only the richest households and institutions like monasteries seem to have been able to afford mortars of metal or a suitable stone such as Purbeck marble (fine Carrara marble also came into use for this purpose, probably in the sixteenth century). Wooden storage vessels such as barrels continued in use right through the medieval period, and wood was also the most common material for plates and bowls. ❼ The survival of any wooden artefact is always dependent on exceptional circumstances of preservation – and they were always prone to being used as fuel after they had come to the end of their useful life – so they are relatively rare.

Left Reconstruction of a mosiac found in Gresham Street; **Right** Roman ceramic lamp showing a bird on a pomegranate branch

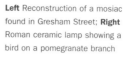

Elaborately painted fragment of Roman wall plaster with a tromp l'oeil depiction of columns and garlands

Furnishings

Roman houses were sparsely furnished with couches, tables, folding stools and cupboards. Wealthy establishments had walls painted with simple ① or more elaborate designs ② and floors decorated with mosaics, one of the most exciting discoveries an archaeologist can make. ③ Windows were glazed, shuttered or barred, and heating was provided in the principal rooms by an underfloor hypocaust system. Humbler dwellings made do with wooden or beaten-earth floors and hearths and braziers.

Artificial lighting was provided by candles, torches or oil-lamps made of copper alloy, pottery and iron. Lamps, which used imported olive oil for fuel, were sometimes suspended from a wall or beam. Pottery lamps, imported from the continent, often had distinctive pictorial designs, ④ and novelty designs were also popular. ⑤ Most lamps were small and relatively inefficient and were not generally used in London after

the end of the second century, perhaps because of disruption to the supply of olive oil. It is probable that candles or tallows were used instead, set in candlesticks or simply stuck to improvised bases.

Most evidence for Roman furniture comes from tomb reliefs as surviving examples are rare. Tables made of Kimmeridge shale from Dorset were fashionable, and archaeologists have recovered a leg and tabletop made of this material.

Iconographic evidence, supplemented by examples found elsewhere in the Roman empire, shows that couches and seats were often decorated with elaborate metal mounts. A lively leaping panther ⑥ from 1 Poultry may be such an attachment. Wooden furniture would have been made more comfortable by mattresses and cushions.

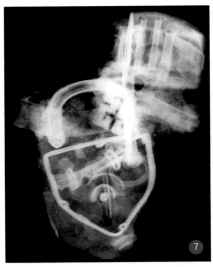

Left With the aid of X-radiography it is possible to see the internal workings of this medieval padlock; **Below left** A Roman copper alloy key for a rotary lock, worn as a ring; **Above** This iron padlock and two rotary keys were amongst a remarkable assemblage of 16th-century security equipment found in Southwark at London Bridge; **Right** A fuming pot, used to burn aromatic herbs

Above An ornate lead tripod candlestick; **Below** A late 16th-century chimney mantle dressed from Reigate Stone, a late example of this tradition of fireplace construction that originated in the medieval period

In the medieval period locks and security equipment ⑦ seem to have been made by accomplished blacksmiths rather than specialised craftsmen, even though the best products required some of the most demandingly precise work. Conversely, what amounts almost to a craft conspiracy emerges from a survey of excavated locks and keys. Several keys have been found with elaborate notching, which has no corresponding complexity among the mechanisms occasionally preserved in locks. An exaggeratedly and visibly ornate tool appears to have turned hidden internal workings that were routinely very simple. This presumably impressed a buyer that the lock on sale was extremely complicated, and therefore worth more than might otherwise have been thought.

Lighting was provided in a number of different ways in medieval London. Candlesticks made of several different materials were available, as were iron

spikes from the twelfth to fourteenth centuries, highly decorated tripods of lead ⑧ or tin in the twelfth and thirteenth centuries, and plainer pewter and copper alloy ones from the later medieval period onwards. These supplemented oil-lamps, initially ceramic and then in the later medieval period glass, that hung from chains, though such lamps appear to have been largely confined to the homes of the rich and to wealthy institutions. Ceramic candlesticks were a post-medieval development.

Furniture was uncommon in the medieval period, and when no longer serviceable it might have served as fuel. This in part explains why very little has been recovered, even in waterlogged areas where wooden items might survive. Part of a simple stool dates to the twelfth century ⑨ and a sixteenth-century oak panel with gothic-style blind arcading is a very rare survival from an unusually decorative item, found discarded behind the river wall in Southwark.

Above Fragment of finely made leather garment; **Below left** Part of a Venus figurine, with elaborately curled hair

Clothing

Some flavour of the variety of dress seen in first-century Roman London can be appreciated in a typical street scene. ❶ The formal dress of a Roman male citizen was the voluminous toga, but normal daywear in London would have consisted of a short tunic and cloak or hooded cape, fastened on each shoulder with a brooch – brightly coloured examples were made from copper alloy and enamel. ❷ Despite depictions of scantily clad goddesses, women dressed modestly, wearing tunics and all-enveloping mantles. Apart from leather shoes and laced sandals, which are frequent finds in waterlogged rubbish deposits, examples of actual dress rarely survive. Remarkable exceptions are the fragments of textiles made of wool and silk found in the burial of a woman dating to the fourth century in the northern Roman cemetery at Spitalfields.

Contemporary illustrations, such as that of a young woman on a lead medallion, show draped figures with elaborate hairstyles. ❸ A late first-century pin would have been used to create a high-swept hairstyle, and simple bone and copper alloy hairpins ❹ are common finds in excavations of the Roman period, with jet becoming popular in the third and fourth centuries. Combs made of wood and, later, composite antler were used to dress the hair.

Soldiers must have been frequent sights on the streets of Londinium, and parts of their distinctive dress are often found. Examples include fragments of scale armour from a first-century waterfront deposit and a fine fourth-century chip-carved belt set, ❺ which, although military in style, may in fact have been worn by an official in late Roman London.

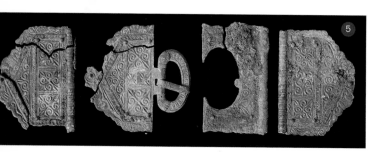

Left The tombstone of a legionary soldier gives an indication of male dress; **Right** Roman military-type fittings and brooch recovered from layers under the seating of the amphitheatre, perhaps lost by soldiers in the audience

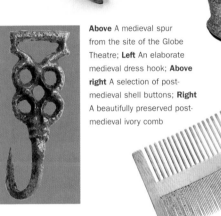

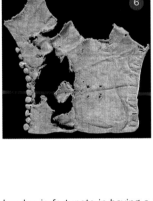

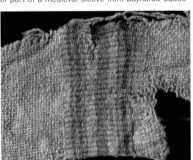

Left The cheek-piece from a helmet dated to the end of the 16th century, and found in Southwark; **Above** A late 14th-century pouch made from a half silk velvet with a tablet woven edge; **Below** Detail of part of a medieval sleeve from Baynards Castle

Above A medieval spur from the site of the Globe Theatre; **Left** An elaborate medieval dress hook; **Above right** A selection of post-medieval shell buttons; **Right** A beautifully preserved post-medieval ivory comb

London is fortunate in having a significant number of fragments of medieval textiles, and to a lesser extent later leather garments, which come from excavations of waterlogged deposits along the waterfront. These include several pieces of medieval sleeves 6 as well as neck openings from tunic-type clothing which have dense rows of buttons and corresponding holes along the openings. The buttons are made of bunched fabric covered with textile and sewn into a tight roundel. Other rare clothing survivals are knee garters and a small number of incomplete hoods – one with the fashionable narrow

tubular extension which hung down the back, known as a liripipe. Even more remarkable is a hair extension, partly of silk and partly of human hair – a device used in the stiff plaits that created a frame around women's faces, as seen in many contemporary representations of the fourteenth century. From somewhat later are substantial fragments of sixteenth- and early seventeenth-century leather jackets, decorated with ornate slashed and pierced patterns.

Shoes seem to have undergone a major transformation around the beginning of the

fourteenth century. A more standardised fitting than the previous individual cut was introduced, corresponding with a change to closer-fitting, figure-hugging styles evident in other elements of clothing. From the late 1300s, among examples of many other medieval footwear fashions, are some of the leather shoes known as *poulaines*, with their exaggeratedly elongated toe ends. 7 In contrast to these, the late fifteenth and early sixteenth centuries saw the introduction of greatly broadened toes, taking fashion to another extreme.

Left A 17th-century leather shoe from the Rose Theatre in Southwark; **Far left** Medieval pattens or overshoes worn to protect footwear in London's muddy streets; **Right** Two late medieval leather shoes with narrow *poulaine* toes which would have been filled with moss to keep them rigid

Amber beads from the necklace of a Bronze Age woman whose burial was discovered during the construction of a new rail track into London

A Roman enamelled brooch in the form of a stag

Above left A Roman brooch; **Right** A Roman 'key' ring; **Below** An enamelled head stud brooch with chain from the site at Poultry, typical of the costume jewellery of the 2nd century

Above A Roman intaglio from Southwark

Jewellery

Jewellery was both functional and fashionable, and worn by men and women.

Roman men and women wore brooches, primarily as functional dress fasteners, although some appear to be purely decorative. One example in the form of a crouching hare is decorated with niello inlay typical of the first century AD. **1** Bold brooch designs were fashionable, often with brightly coloured enamel decoration.

Men wore little other jewellery, which was considered effeminate, but signet rings set with engraved intaglios were worn as personal seals or amulets, and could indicate status. In the Republican period (up to 31 BC) gold jewellery could be worn only by members of the aristocracy, although the rules were later relaxed. An early second-century intaglio depicting Alexander the Great **2** may have belonged to a soldier, while a fabulous creature composed of a cockerel, horse and satyr has symbolism associated with the god Bacchus. **3**

Women wore necklaces, earrings, finger rings and bracelets. An expensive and delicate gold and emerald necklace **4** is a type that was often copied in copper alloy and glass. Heavy necklaces composed of elaborate glass 'melon' beads **5** have also been found in London, and, most

Early 3rd-century enamelled brooch, gold-in-glass bead and gold and iron finger rings

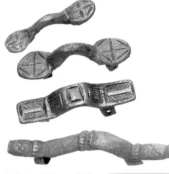

Left top Antler mould for an 8th-century disc brooch showing a standing bird with a border of ring-and-dot motifs. The channel for pouring in the metal alloy can be seen at the top; Left A 9th-century glass bead with inlaid twisted rope decoration from the site of the Royal Opera House

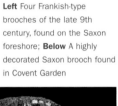

Left Four Frankish-type brooches of the late 9th century, found on the Saxon foreshore; Below A highly decorated Saxon brooch found in Covent Garden

Medieval gold rings with semi-precious stones from excavations on the waterfront

unusually, one composed of wooden beads which was preserved by being charred in the Boudican fire. The first-century AD Roman author Pliny records the popularity of pearls, and one set in an elaborate gold earring was found in the amphitheatre. ⑥ Other excavated earrings are usually plain, often hoops, made mostly of copper alloy and more rarely of gold. Simple bracelets made from copper alloy wire came in a variety of styles, and bangles carved from shale and jet were fashionable, especially in the third and fourth centuries.

By far the greatest number of medieval items of personal adornment recovered are made of base metals, with decorative gems, if any, imitated in glass. ⑦ Copper alloys, used for virtually every category of accessory, were sometimes made to look more splendid by gilding or coating with tin or silver. Pewter jewellery is surprisingly common, and this metal was used extensively for brooches and mounts in the medieval period. Towards the end of that era highly decorative buckles are also found in pewter, though this cheaper alternative to copper and iron tended to have a built-in obsolescence due to the alloy's weakness. From the highly accomplished openwork souvenir brooches for pilgrims of the

fourteenth and fifteenth centuries, ⑧ a marked decline in inspiration seems to set in during the first half of the sixteenth century, a result of the growing political force of the Reformation. This culminated in what appears to be a sudden and complete halt in the centuries-old tradition of lead/tin jewellery around the mid 1500s.

In contrast, the first half of the sixteenth century was the high point of superficially complicated and showy but cheap accessories of copper alloy wire, and also saw a new line of decorative hooked tags in great variety. The post-medieval period, while producing some fine finger rings and other accessories, seems from archaeological evidence to have been a time when mainstream artistic developments were less in evidence in jewellery at the lower end of the market than at this same social level throughout the medieval period. Renaissance motifs are almost completely absent in the buckles of the sixteenth century, while strapends and mounts, long the items with the most elaborate ornamentation, virtually disappeared from the repertoire.

Out on the town

This large prehistoric vessel, with a capacity of about four pints, was found in the Thames. Made of oak staves covered in bronze, it was probably used for communal drinking at feasts

1 A fragment of pottery showing a heavily armed gladiator

A Roman oil-lamp decorated with a scene of dancers

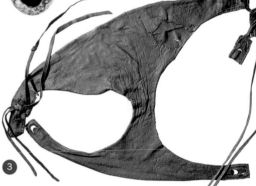

2

3

Entertainment

Games of all kinds were popular in London in the past – some are still familiar today.

Public spectacles in Roman London were held in the amphitheatre, where gladiatorial combat and wild beast shows were staged – both frequent themes on pottery vessels **1** and lamps. Glass cups and lamps also commemorate the equally popular sport of chariot racing. Roman London's theatre building has yet to be located, but many objects from the city have some reference to the stage. A copper alloy mount features a comic mask, while an iron finger ring is set with a seal depicting Thalia, the Muse of Comedy. **2** A lamp originally from Gaul shows a pair of stave dancers and an actual leather 'bikini' may have been worn by a female acrobat. **3** There is little direct evidence for musicians in London, but one pipe from a copper alloy tibia and a tuning peg from a lyre have been found.

To judge from the large numbers of dice and counters found by archaeologists in London, the Romans appear to have been addicted to gaming and gambling. The Roman poet Ovid certainly considered the playing of board games to be an essential feminine accomplishment. Most dice were very similar to modern ones, with values marked by ring-and-dot motifs and the opposite sides adding up to seven. A most unusual die from Southwark **4** has letters to mark the values, and not only do they total seven on opposite faces, they also make complete words. Counters **5** came in bone, glass or pottery, the latter recycled from vessels. One lucky individual was buried with a full gaming set, complete with box.

Gambling seems to have been equally popular in medieval times, **6** though gaming counters of antler for use on boards are more common in the earlier part of the period than towards its end. Dice were in

4 **Above** An unusual Roman stone die with carved letters in place of spots. Unfortunately no-one has yet worked out how such dice were used

5

6 A medieval tooled leather gaming cup and dice

Top A child's rattle made from a shell trapped within a decorative lead sphere; **Left** A toy made from a piece of antler, found within one of the 12th-century buildings at the Guildhall; **Right** Pewter dolls of late Tudor date

Left A medieval whistle in the form of a dog's head with 'Ave Maria' moulded along both sides; **Below** Medieval panpipes found on Upper Thames Street still produced a musical flute-like sound

use throughout the medieval and later periods. Usually of bone, they seem to have become more standardised (so that the numbers on opposite faces add up to seven) around the sixteenth century, when legislation to outlaw gambling was being introduced – a sure sign that the practice was flourishing.

Toys, in the sense of miniatures intended for children's play, seem to have appeared around the twelfth century, with mass production of lead and tin mounted knights in full swing by 1300. **7** Tiny versions of jugs for the table were presumably for girls, while toy soldiers for boys continued in favour up to the sixteenth century. Human figures from the end of the Tudor era include a remarkable series of accurately dressed pewter women and men. Small bone daggers carved to resemble the real thing became a favourite plaything around

this time. The repertoire of miniature toy kitchenware **8** and serving vessels of pewter increased markedly in the seventeenth century, and a range of other household accessories came in. A few plates and pieces of furniture were dated and marked with the makers' initials in the 1640s, giving us some fixed points for dating. By the end of the 1600s coaches, warships, watches and (in copper alloy) guns that could actually fire **9** were also established as playthings. There was still room, however, for simple noise-making items like whizzers cut from sheet lead, and whistles.

Below A very rare early medieval horn with finger holes; **Left** A bridge from a stringed instrument and three tuning pegs found in an 11th-century building at Guildhall

Roman baths

The Romans had a passion for bathing, and Londinium contained its fair share of facilities for this activity, both public and private.

The grand scale, architectural complexity and technological innovation of public baths made them a key element of civic pride across the Empire, comparable to the great railway termini of the Victorian age or the shopping malls of today. Very few Roman Londoners had homes with piped water or sewage connections, making the public bath an essential amenity for all classes and groups, including travellers and people on visits from the country.

A set of baths discovered at Huggin Hill, in the heart of the Roman city in 1964, and extensively excavated in 1969 and 1989, are by far the largest in Roman London. ① Built in about AD 70, they commanded the riverfront just upstream from the port, and were a visible product of Roman technology and achievement – important messages to convey just ten years after Boudica's revolt. The main range included changing rooms, and cold, warm and hot baths – the latter (a caldarium) was at the western end.

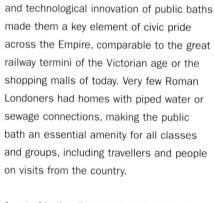

Right A comb and manicure set from Pudding Lane and London Wall. The bone comb has a choice of wide and fine teeth. The manicure set consists of five implements for personal hygiene, including tweezers, a nail-file and a scoop for using cosmetics, and would have been suspended from a belt

Above Working on the hypocaust in the tepidarium (warm bath) of the Billingsgate bathhouse, which has been preserved beneath modern buildings

Above Apsidal-ended bath faced with white tesserae with a thin band of orange tesserae around the foot of the wall above the watertight quarter-round moulding; such elaborate baths are relatively rare in Britain

Lightweight tile-and-concrete vaulting was used in the construction of the halls, which were elaborately decorated. The main heated rooms incorporated heating ducts beneath the floors (hypocausts) **2** and within the walls, served by furnaces in a wing to the north. Water cisterns and reservoirs were fed by hillside springs.

The Huggin Hill baths were altered frequently during their short life, and expanded to meet the demands of a growing population. Once two caldaria were built, the baths could offer separate bathing for men and women without restricting the hours of use (the Emperor Hadrian had banned mixed bathing in *c.* AD 117). Late afternoon and early evening were the preferred bathing times – when the water was hottest. Staff helped people in and out of the plunge baths and served as masseurs, perfumers and attendants. Other staff operated the furnaces and supplied fuel and water.

After only half a century of use the Huggin Hill baths were systematically demolished. High maintenance costs, second-century economic uncertainties and population decline may have proved too much for the municipality or public subscription to bear. Lead pipes, marble veneers and other salvageable items were stripped from the building.

Eleven other London bath sites have been identified, including the late first-century Cheapside baths, which may have been associated with an inn. **3** London's later Roman baths were mainly suites in private or commercial buildings. Excavations at Poultry in 1995 uncovered an early third-century stone building at the rear of a roadside property, which was modified after AD 299 to include a hypocaust system and a hot plunge bath. **4** At Pudding Lane, near the Thames bridgehead, a fine plunge bath **5** and a latrine were found in an inn or luxurious private residence. Just to the

east, the Billingsgate bathhouse had a small bathing suite located in a courtyard area, probably an afterthought to the main house whose wings enclosed it. **6** And excavations in Southwark in 1983 revealed a large late Roman building with an opulent bathing suite, possibly the private rooms and offices of an important official or his staff. **7**

The evidence from London suggests that the physical provision and social context of the baths changed over time, with private and neighbourhood baths replacing the large public baths, reflecting a growth in personal modesty and a widening social gap between wealthy and poor.

The amphitheatre

The largest and most impressive building in Londinium was the amphitheatre.

Right A small bronze figurine dressed as a Samnite gladiator, wearing a helmet with mask and holding a square shield on his left arm. His right arm may have held a sword or dagger but this is now missing; **Below** The image of a fallen gladiator on an oil-lamp and gladiators in combat on a sherd of imported pottery found at the Guildhall amphitheatre

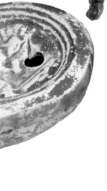

It had long been suspected that Londinium might have had an amphitheatre, but it was only as recently as 1988 that archaeologists digging beneath the courtyard of the Guildhall finally found it. As the largest of all the Roman public buildings, and the place where gladiatorial combats and other events were staged, this was one of the most significant finds in London's archaeology. Fragments of it had in fact already been found in the past, but they had not been identified as belonging to the amphitheatre. It was only with the discovery of the curving walls of the eastern end ❶ that finally archaeologists knew they had discovered what they had long been searching for.

London's amphitheatre was originally built shortly after AD 70, a few years after the Boudican rebellion which destroyed the city. At first it was a timber structure, with an arena dug into the natural gravels and surrounded by 10 to 15 tiers of wooden benches for seating. The arena surface was of soft sand over a firmer bedding of gravel. In the early second century AD the amphitheatre was enlarged and improved by rebuilding both the wall around the arena and the flanking entranceways in stone and tile, ❷ while the superstructure, seating, external wall and extensive subsurface drainage continued as timber structures. We can calculate the area of the structure as being about 100 m by

Above An archaeologist cleaning the masonry of the doorway into the chamber for wild animals. The mortices cut into the threshold stones for the support beams of the sliding trapdoor can be seen on either side of the doorway

85 m – an amphitheatre of this size may have held an audience of about 5000 spectators, at a time when the population of Londinium was probably between 20,000 and 30,000. It was tiny in comparison to the Colosseum in Rome, which may have held as many as 50,000 people, but it would certainly have been the most impressive Roman building in the city. 3

Gladiatorial combats seem to have had their origin in the fourth century BC in ritualised combats associated with private funerals. The first recorded public showing of gladiators was in 264 BC in Rome. At some time during the first century BC, gladiatorial combats became part of the regular games that were held to celebrate religious festivals. 4 It was also at this time that permanent arenas were built to stage the combats. Under the emperors, gladiator fighting became increasingly popular as a public entertainment in the first and second centuries AD. Shows were funded by rich dignitaries looking for favour from the masses, and in the provinces by the Emperor's officials.

Shows in London would probably have included the killing of large numbers of 'criminals' or prisoners of war, wild animal fights and, as the highlight, individual combats between professional gladiators.

Amphitheatres and gladiators were a key part of Roman society, with a mass appeal comparable to that of some sports today. Many of the gladiators were slaves or convicted criminals and the majority died in the arena, though some became major celebrities – a few retiring free and rich.

Gladiatorial fighting continued elsewhere in the Empire until the end of the fourth century but appears to have ended earlier in Britain, at a time when other large public buildings were also falling out of use. There is still much debate about the role of the new Roman state religion, Christianity, in its end. Much of London's amphitheatre was systematically dismantled, and by the early fifth century little of this huge feat of engineering was still visible apart from a grassed-over hollow in the ground.

Right Part of a small Roman oil-lamp decorated with a boar; **Below** A lead 'curse' found in the amphitheatre, here unrolled. The short inscription is probably the name of a gladiator, and the four corner holes show that it had been nailed to a wall

Above Many street names in London still reflect earlier activities – Bear Gardens reminds us of the five bearbaiting arenas thought to have existed in the area of Bankside

Theatres

Archaeologists have discovered several of the theatres where Shakespeare's plays were first performed.

Below Dame Peggy Ashcroft and Dustin Hoffman joined those protesting about potential destruction of the Rose Theatre's remains; **Below right** Excavations in progress on the site

We are not certain whether Roman London was provided with a theatre, although it seems probable. A few excavated finds, including a copper alloy mount in the form of a theatrical mask, **1** hint that such a building may yet be found.

In the medieval period, centres for what were regarded as disreputable pursuits had grown up in areas beyond the control of the City authorities. One of these was Bankside, on the south side of the Thames, which by the sixteenth century was a thriving community devoted to the entertainment of Londoners. It was packed with taverns, brothels, gambling dens and animal baiting rings, two of which are shown in an engraving of 1560–90. **2**

Existing buildings were sometimes adapted for plays or cockfights, but soon purpose-built theatres were constructed for the large audiences keen to see the new plays being produced. In 1989, archaeologists made one of London's most spectacular discoveries – the Rose Theatre, built for Philip Henslowe in 1587. **3** The threatened destruction of the remains of the theatre where many of Shakespeare's most famous plays had first been performed caused a

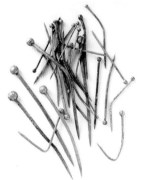

Above Tudor and contemporary European coins and tokens from the site of the Rose Theatre;
Right An assortment of pins found at the Rose

Above A gold ring found during excavations of the second yard surface of the Rose. The motto on the ring is in French and translates as 'Think of me, God willing';
Left A token found at the site of the Globe Theatre, dated 1625 and with the initials of the maker R W on the reverse

national and international outcry, with the public, archaeologists, actors and the theatrical profession fighting to see such a rare and tangible part of our literary heritage preserved beneath the new buildings on the site. **4** Government intervention ensured its survival.

The theatre was a polygonal building with perhaps 12 or 14 sides. Its timber-framed walls rested on brick and stone foundations and supported the three-storey galleries with seating. The enclosed inner yard, for cheaper standing room, was open to the sky. The building was substantially remodelled, probably in 1592, when it was extended to increase the capacity of the yard. This was re-floored with a layer of clinker and crushed hazelnuts – perhaps the remains of snacks eaten during the performances. **5** Debris from the demolition of the building, thought to have taken place between 1603 and 1605, included fragments of the lath and plaster panels which infilled the timber frame, as well as thatch from the roof. Many other finds illustrate aspects of the life of the playhouse, from pottery money boxes **6** used to collect the entrance fees to a turtle shell (from an exotic meal or a stage prop?).

Archaeologists have also uncovered fragments of London's other Tudor theatres, including the Hope, again built for Phillip Henslowe in 1613–14, and the most famous of all – the Globe. **7** This was built in 1599 for Richard and Cuthbert Burbage, William Shakespeare, John Hemings, Augustine Phillips, Thomas Pope and William Kemp. It survived until destroyed by fire in 1613. Rebuilt the following year, it was demolished shortly after the closure of the London playhouses by order of the Puritan parliament in 1642. A small excavated fragment of the Globe was enough to confirm the presence of a polygonal building with brick foundations for external stair turrets, as shown on some contemporary illustrations. The site of this playhouse has also been preserved in situ.

These sites form our only direct physical link with the context in which the plays of Shakespeare, Marlowe and their contemporaries were first performed and have proved of immense interest to archaeologists, historians, students of English literature and language, actors and the wider public.

Above The reconstructed Globe Theatre in Southwark;
Below Archaeologists recording the brick walls of what is thought to be the Hope Theatre, built in 1613–14

Religion

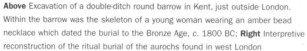

Above Excavation of a double-ditch round barrow in Kent, just outside London. Within the barrow was the skeleton of a young woman wearing an amber bead necklace which dated the burial to the Bronze Age, *c.* 1800 BC; **Right** Interpretive reconstruction of the ritual burial of the aurochs found in west London

Prehistoric ritual

Archaeologists now recognise the difficulties in attempting to differentiate between 'ritual' and 'domestic' activity in the remains they discover, particularly before the advent of written records. It is probable, in fact, that for the early inhabitants of what is now Greater London such a clear-cut division would have been meaningless. Nevertheless, from the Neolithic period onwards, archaeological remains indicate the importance of ritual activities in the daily lives of the prehistoric population.

On a small scale, archaeologists have found pits in west London containing what appear to be deliberately stacked sherds of pottery decorated with incised lines, known as grooved ware. **1** Accompanying these sherds were flint tools and food remains, especially hazelnuts, as well as sloes and crab apples. Were these the remains of feasts held to celebrate festivals or marriages?

Crop marks are the lines of ancient buried features visible in crops when photographed from the air due to differences in growth. Such marks revealed the existence of an enclosure, probably a Neolithic 'causewayed enclosure', on the edge of a gravel ridge, looking out over the Thames valley. It measured some 250 m across and consisted of two concentric ditches 5 to 6 m wide, interrupted by causeways. Perhaps this was used as a seasonal meeting-place for bartering, marriages and other feasts and

Above left The high quality of some of the objects apparently deliberately deposited in the Thames, such as the 'Battersea shield' suggests that there must have been considerable ritual involved; **Left** Skeleton of an adult horse found in Kent. The burial is of Iron Age date and its content indicated it was probably of ritual significance; **Right** Cremation urns dating to 2000–1500 BC found in west London

celebrations. Ring ditches, which probably surrounded Early Bronze Age round barrows also show up as crop marks along this ridge. ② Archaeologists found one such ditch next to the Thames, encircling an urn containing the cremated remains of two adults.

The Stanwell Cursus is the largest prehistoric monument found in London. ③ Thought to have been a processional way along which ritual ceremonies would have moved, it runs through the landscape for more than 3.7 km and must have been a highly visible feature of western London from about 3000 to 1000 BC. It was identified from crop marks that traced the lines of the ditches which flanked a raised central bank, and sections have been excavated.

The dismembered remains of an aurochs (a type of large wild ox, now extinct) found

in a pit ④ perhaps represent a continuation of the tradition of ritually burying 'special' deposits. Accompanying the bones were six Early Bronze Age barbed-and-tanged flint arrowheads, either from the hunt in which the animal was killed, or symbols of that event.

Such overt monumental evidence for ceremonial activities disappears during the Middle and Late Bronze Age, but 'ritual activity' from these times is represented by the bronze swords, spearheads and daggers recovered from the River Thames, mostly deliberately cast into the water as offerings. Human skulls from the Thames, radiocarbon-dated to the same period, suggest that the metalwork may have been deposited during funerary rites. Cremations of this period are found in pottery urns, often inverted over the burnt remains, either in small groups or larger cemeteries.

The practice of throwing metalwork into the Thames as offerings to the gods continued during the Iron Age. Such splendid objects as the ceremonial helmet from Waterloo and the Battersea shield, ⑤ as well as a number of swords and daggers, have been recovered from the river. A probable temple of this period was found by archaeologists at Heathrow. ⑥ An inner foundation trench and outer rectangle of posts, measuring approximately 9 by 11 m, were traced, with posts for an entrance porch at one end. While this is the only such building known from the London area, this unusual plan is known from a few examples from elsewhere in Britain and there are others on the continent.

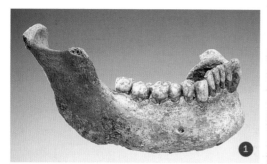

Above top A jawbone from an early Roman burial with a coin wedged behind its teeth, presumably to pay the ferryman Charon to transport the deceased to the underworld

Above Limestone finial from a Roman mausoleum in Southwark, in the shape of a pinecone, a symbol of the god Atys and often associated with funerary monuments

Roman ritual

A bewildering diversity of religions was practised in London during the Roman period, a result of the huge area conquered by the Romans and the influences of the numerous cults of the inhabitants. Various religions were transported throughout the Empire and became immensely popular far from their original home. In addition to the widespread worship of the traditional Roman deities, eastern mystery religions such as Mithraism and, of course, towards the end of the Roman period, Christianity, found many followers.

A green jasper intaglio, probably from a 1st-century ring, depicting a four-horse chariot driven by Sol, the Roman sun god, who crossed the sky daily as he travelled between his two magnificent palaces in the eastern and western portions of the sky

Above left The head of Serapis, made from marble in Italy, was among a number of sculptures found within the Temple of Mithras; **Above** The head of Mithras, wearing his traditional cap, and the figure of a water-deity, with a view over the temple looking towards the apsidal west end

Above Figurines of Venus were popular in household shrines. These examples came from graves where they may represent some belief in afterlife and regeneration, associated with the legend of Venus' birth from sea foam; **Left** A headless pipeclay figurine of Minerva, goddess of wisdom and patron of arts and trade. Found near Newgate, she may have originally stood in a shrine by the City wall

Evidence for Roman religion and ritual is found in many forms across the London region. Although the number of religious structures or actual temples known is quite small, numerous traces of religious practices tell us much about the attitudes and beliefs of Roman Londoners. ❶ One ritual was the apparently deliberate depositing of elaborate metalwork in the River Walbrook. And whole pots and even dead dogs were thrown into disused wells in Southwark. Often the pots had holes intentionally made in them, as for example one found in a well just north of the city in Spitalfields. Were the people trying to appease earth spirits for having disturbed them?

The siting of Roman temples and religious precincts in London is open to much debate. There was possibly a concentration on the west side of the city, south of where St Paul's Cathedral now stands, and there were undoubtedly some religious structures outside the walls. One lay in Greenwich Park, at the point where the Roman road

dives down the hillside before approaching the settlement at Southwark. A structure found beneath the Old Bailey, which would have been immediately outside the walls, may also have been a temple. And a third possible example, built in about AD 100, was found by archaeologists in Southwark alongside Watling Street, ❷ again outside the settlement. It stood within the Roman cemetery and nearby were two walled areas and a mausoleum, suggesting that the dead buried here were of a high status indeed. One of the burials was probably marked by a monument adorned with a head, either of the god Pan or Silenus – a rare and spectacular find. ❸ And the cremated remains of one woman were buried with a group of tazze (cups) and lamps, ❹ one of which was decorated with a gladiator; some archaeologists think she may even have been a gladiator herself.

London's most famous Roman temple is the Temple of Mithras, ❺ excavated in the 1950s and now reconstructed on Queen

Victoria Street. The temple lay on the east side of the River Walbrook and dominated what was probably a rather boggy valley. It was built in about AD 250 and originally consisted of a rectangular stone structure with an apse at its eastern end; its interior was divided into three aisles by two rows of seven columns built on low walls. Numerous alterations were made to the structure and a narthex, or entrance hall, was added in the fourth century. At this time the temple is thought to have been used by followers of Bacchus (the god of wine), perhaps indicating that the worship of Mithras was in decline – an interpretation apparently confirmed by the fact that also around this period a group of sculptures, including the famous head of a statue of Mithras himself, was buried beneath the earth floors of the building.

Right This 1st-century beaker from the Nene Valley was recovered from a Roman burial in Southwark

Roman law forbade the burial of the dead within cities and so the commonest site for cemeteries was alongside the roads which led out of settlements. **1** This was true of all the major highways out of London, and several other settlements. Burials lay alongside the roads that ran out of Southwark, and the settlement at Bow, on the banks of the River Lea, also had a burial ground.

Reflecting the great variety of beliefs and cultures in the Roman Empire, burial practices were also very diverse. The two main methods of disposing of the dead were inhumation (burial of the body) and cremation. Both were practised in the Roman period in Britain, with cremations

tending to be less common in the third and fourth centuries AD.

The dead were probably cremated on funeral pyres within the cemetery and their ashes were afterwards placed in some kind of vessel. **2** Archaeologists have found many different receptacles used in this way, varying from small ceramic jars to reused amphorae (storage jars) **3** and beautiful glass urns, specifically made for the purpose.

Inhumation burials also varied. In the early part of the Roman period bodies were buried aligned from south to north, while in the later Roman period they were more frequently interred from west to east. It was

not only Christians who were buried in this way; followers of Mithras, for example, were also laid from west to east.

The wealth of an individual would, to a large extent, govern the container in which his or her remains were placed. Most were buried in a simple wooden coffin **4** held together by nails. One common practice was to place a layer of chalk in the coffin. **5** The wealthiest few might be able to afford a more elaborate container. One of the most exciting and dramatic finds in recent years came from Spitalfields, **6** where an ornate lead coffin placed inside a stone tomb or sarcophagus was found to contain the skeleton of a woman of about 25 years of age **7** – the first such discovery in London

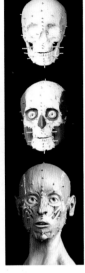

Left The opening of the sarcophagus was carried out in a carefully controlled envionment; **Above and above right** The face of the woman from the sarcophagus was reconstructed by experts; **Below** The scallop shell motif used as decoration on the lid of the sarcophagus was often used in association with burials

for 125 years. Analysis of the woman's DNA suggested that she was born in southern Europe, possibly Spain. **8** She had obviously been very wealthy indeed and had been buried with a group of fine glass phials **9** and jet grave goods. Thousands queued to see her tomb when it was moved to the Museum of London.

Many Roman burials were accompanied by grave goods – either personal items of importance to the individual buried, offerings of food or drink to be taken by the dead on their journey into the afterlife, or artefacts which would have been used during the burial ceremony itself. Food offerings might consist of an animal such as a chicken, sometimes buried in a pot.

Drinks may have been placed in glass vessels **10** or in ceramic pots, and glass phials may have contained ointments or perfumes for pouring over the coffin during the burial ceremony. Personal items of jewellery, often made of jet **11** or shale, are frequent finds, and include necklaces, bracelets and mirrors.

A jet pendant depicting the head of the gorgon Medusa

Left London viewed from Southwark in about 1650, before its destruction in the Great Fire. St Paul's is on the left of the picture and Southwark Cathedral is in the foreground, and the skyline is bristling with the spires of London's many churches; **Above** A fragment of wall-painting, originally thought to be from the medieval church of St Nicholas Acon but more likely to be a 19th-century fake

Places of worship

Today there are many thousands of parishes in London. Originally it was probably served by a few very large parishes, which extended beyond the City until the great expansion of London and its population after 1600.

Above The remains of St Benet Sherehog found beneath 1 Poultry; **Right** Successive mortar floorings at St Benet's church had raised the internal area by over a metre by the 13th century; **Far right** Archaeologists clean and record the damaged floor of medieval St Ethelburga's

St Dunstan's Stepney once covered much of the area of east London outside the City, and St Margaret's Westminster formerly stretched all the way from there to Kingsway and Oxford Street. Eventually new parishes were created by subdividing the larger ones, such as Christchurch Spitalfields out of St Dunstan's, and St Martin in the Fields out of St Margaret's.

Numerous small parishes also grew up in the City as individuals or groups of people in one street or block decided that they wanted their own church and their own priest – and had the money to pay for them. This led to the creation of the enormous number of parishes (over 100) in such a small area, and panoramas of London's skyline from the sixteenth and seventeenth centuries are dominated by church spires. ❶ Numerous churches were built in the later eleventh and twelfth centuries as the population grew, though some were very small and had no attached burial grounds. Most were destroyed in the Great Fire of

1666, but archaeologists occasionally have the opportunity to excavate a few, such as St Benet Sherehog ❷ and St Nicholas Shambles. Typically they were simple stone churches with earth floors, ❸ although wealthier parishes might add new aisles to cater for a larger congregation and to exhibit their wealth and piety. The foundations of St Mary Aldermanbury – the structure of which was moved to the USA – can still be seen and reveal a similar plan. Of the churches that were rebuilt after the Great Fire, some were of the highest quality, such as St Stephen Walbrook. Many more of London's churches were destroyed during the bombing raids by the German Luftwaffe in the Second World War. Medieval churches do survive in areas that were once villages outside London, such as Stepney. Repairs allow the recording of parts of these surviving structures, such as St Mary at Hill in the City, and disasters make emergency recording essential, such as after the fire at St Mary Barnes and the destruction of St Ethelburga by an IRA bomb. ❹

By far the majority of London's churches were built in the eighteenth, nineteenth and twentieth centuries, as London's population increased dramatically. Some very fine examples include the churches of the architect Nicholas Hawksmoor dating from the early eighteenth century, such as Christchurch Spitalfields ❺ and St Anne's Limehouse. Excavations in church crypts are sometimes carried out, as at Christchurch Spitalfields and St Lawrence Jewry. ❻

Christianity is not the only religion represented in medieval London's buried past. Until 1290, when its members were expelled, a large Jewish community lived in London. Their burial ground lay outside the walls, where the Museum of London now stands, and a ritual cleansing bath or mikvah ❼ has been found in the area named old Jewry. This may either have been attached to a synagogue or perhaps a wealthy individual's house.

The Great Drain of Westminster Abbey, found under the Jewel Tower garden at the Palace of Westminster

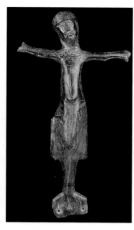

Left This 13th-century figure of Christ crucified was found at Bermondsey Abbey. Decorated with enamel, it was probably once attached to an altar or processional cross and may have been made at Limoges in France; **Below** A souvenir badge depicting the Rood (crucifix) of Bermondsey. The letters on the labels either side of Christ seem to be Latin for 'this is the badge of Bermondsey'. The actual Rood probably dated to the Saxon period and is said to have been discovered near the abbey in 1117. It became a focus of pilgrimage in the medieval period. The badge of lead and tin would have been bought by a pilgrim visiting the shrine

Medieval monastic houses

A variety of monastic houses once formed a significant part of the landscape of London.

Above The walls of the crypt of Wren's St Paul's are constructed largely of the stones from its medieval predecessor which was destroyed in the Great Fire of 1666. Some of the stones have their mouldings revealed, like the 12th-century one shown here; **Below** Measuring a stone decorated in 12th-century style, reused in the wall of St Paul's Cathedral crypt. It would have been part of a doorway in the medieval cathedral

London's medieval religious buildings include numerous monastic houses as well as St Paul's Cathedral, London's only cathedral of the period. All the area south of the Thames in London came under the see of Winchester, though the church at Southwark was only made a cathedral in the early part of the twentieth century. The first mention of a Bishop of London occurs in AD 353, when he is said to have attended the Council of Troyes. A cathedral stood on the site of St Paul's as early as the Saxon period, and after the Norman Conquest it was rebuilt as the largest cathedral in Britain; it also had the tallest spire. Many alterations and additions were made to this structure throughout the centuries, until it was destroyed by the Great Fire in 1666. Wren's wonderful Renaissance cathedral which replaced it ❶ was completed by the early years of the eighteenth century. ❷ The precincts of the medieval cathedral contained many important buildings,

including the bishop's residence and an outdoor pulpit. A school was also founded there which survives to this day.

There was an enormous variety to the monastic buildings in London. Some were colleges for secular canons, such as the cathedral, the chapel of St Stephen in the Palace of Westminster and St Martin-le-Grand, but most were communities of monks, monastic canons or friars who followed one of the various religious rules. One of the most important and wealthy establishments in the country belonged to the Benedictine monks: Westminster Abbey. Founded originally in the Saxon period, it eventually became the royal coronation and burial church and one of the finest building complexes in England. ❸ Archaeologists have also excavated much of the important Cluniac priory at Bermondsey, founded in the late eleventh century, ❹ and many important Augustinian monasteries

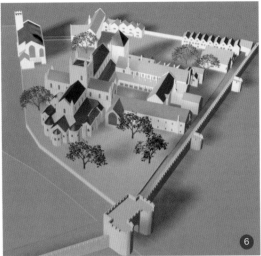

Left Excavations at Merton Priory – looking from the Lady Chapel, through the choir, north transept and north aisle towards the west end; **Right** A group of keys discarded in the infirmary in the late 13th century at St Mary Spital

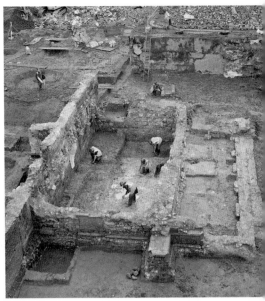

Above top The medieval charnel house and chapel at St Mary Spital; **Above** Reconstruction in about 1500; **Below** Aerial view of excavations of the 15th-century canon's infirmary and adjoining kitchen at St Mary Spital

throughout London. These included Merton Priory, ⑤ which was situated in the countryside, and Holy Trinity Priory, ⑥ which was inside the City. The Augustinians also ran many of the medieval hospitals, such as St Mary Spital, ⑦ St Bartholomew, St Thomas and St Mary Bethlehem (Bedlam). In addition to the church and cloister for the monastic canons, these foundations also had public infirmaries for the sick and destitute. Many of the monastic houses in the City were friaries. Differences in their religious rule – the friars went out into the world preaching rather than leading a life of seclusion – are reflected in the layouts of their churches.

Monastic houses were generally all similar in organisation. The church was at the centre, with a group of buildings clustered around a cloister, usually, though not always, on the south side of the church. On one side of the cloister, frequently over the chapter house, was the dormitory where the monks slept. This usually had a direct connection with the church so that the monks could enter it at night for prayers without going outside. On another side of the cloister was the refectory, or dining hall, with a kitchen nearby. There was often a pulpit in the refectory where a monk would read to his brethren from the scriptures during meal times. Store-rooms and lodgings for the Abbot or Prior and guests occupied the remaining side of the cloister. Numerous other buildings were required to run a monastery, including houses for servants, mills, bakeries, breweries, latrines and even dovecotes. Water-supply and drainage were very important, and each monastery would go to great lengths to ensure it had good provision of both. The finest rooms and the most important areas of the church were sometimes lavishly decorated with tiled floors, sculptures and painted walls.

Above Cistercians return to Stratford Langthorne Abbey after a 450-year absence; **Below** A high-status stone coffin from the north transept of the monastery

Above An outbuilding of the Carthusian monastery at Charterhouse; **Above right** A medieval basement in the precinct of the Nunnery of St Mary de Fonte, Clerkenwell; **Right** A late 15th-century pipe-clay crucifix from Germany or the Netherlands, with traces of paint still showing, found at St Clare's

A medieval wall at St Mary Graces Abbey

Two of the more austere orders were the Cistercians and Carthusians, who preferred secluded sites. The Cistercians were popular in the twelfth century and at this time they founded an abbey at Stratford Langthorne ❶ (on the far side of the River Lea). Two later foundations were the Cistercian Abbey of St Mary Graces ❷ and the Carthusian 'Charterhouse' ❸ – both on the very edge of the City and both on sites of emergency burial grounds for victims of the Black Death. The Carthusians followed a very different rule from the other orders, which was reflected in the layout of their buildings. Rather than having a communal sleeping area, each monk had an individual cell, arranged around a huge cloister, where they spent their time when not in church in silent contemplation.

There were also important female monastic houses in London, including the Augustinian nunnery of St Mary de Fonte in Clerkenwell ❹ and another at Holywell in Shoreditch. Their buildings differ slightly in layout from male monasteries. Parts of their churches were often given over to the local parish, as at St Helen's in the City. The Franciscan nunnery of St Clare was popular with royalty and the nobility; Anne Mowbray, the wife of Richard Duke of York, the younger of the murdered princes in the Tower, was buried there in the late fifteenth century.

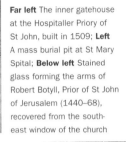

Far left The inner gatehouse at the Hospitaller Priory of St John, built in 1509; **Left** A mass burial pit at St Mary Spital; **Below left** Stained glass forming the arms of Robert Botyll, Prior of St John of Jerusalem (1440–68), recovered from the south-east window of the church

Two unusual but very important monastic houses were those of the Knights Templar at the Temple and Knights Hospitaller at St John's Clerkenwell. The Temple Church still survives, as do the gatehouse, ⑤ crypt and part of the choir of St John's. Both churches originally had round naves when they were built in the twelfth century (St John's was rebuilt in the more traditional rectangular shape at a later date), in imitation of the round nave of the Church of the Holy Sepulchre which the Knights had seen in Jerusalem during the Crusades.

The Temple was closed when the order of the Knights Templar was suppressed in 1312. Most of the other monastic houses survived until the Dissolution of the Monasteries under Henry VIII, between 1535 and 1540. The buildings were generally sold off, demolished or altered, although Westminster Abbey survived to become a cathedral for ten years, and other foundations, such as the nunnery churches, St Mary Overie (now Southwark Cathedral) ⑥ and part of St Bartholomew's, became parish churches. The majority of the monks left without protest, except for Prior John Houghton and some of the monks at the Charterhouse. Prior Houghton was burned at the stake and his arm nailed to the door of the monastery as a warning to the other monks. When they still refused to sign the oath of allegiance, they too were executed.

Above An early 15th-century Canterbury souvenir pilgrim badge, found in Southwark. Southwark Cathedral was the starting point for the pilgrim trail to Canterbury, to visit the shrine of Thomas Becket (St Thomas the Martyr), Archbishop of Canterbury until his murder in 1170 instigated by Henry II

Above Both sides of a lead seal from a papal bulla issued by Pope Gregory XI (1370–78) accompanying a tomb burial found at Spitalfields; **Left** Reconstruction of the 11th-century timber church at St Lawrence Jewry

②

Medieval burial practices

During the medieval period, the majority of people were buried in their local parish cemetery. The monks or nuns, lay brothers, servants and benefactors of a monastic community were interred in the monastery's cemetery, while yet others were buried in cemeteries of hospitals.

Burial within a stone-lined grave in the north transept at Merton Priory, with the hands clasped around a leather belt

Most bodies in a Christian cemetery were laid out in the same way – on their backs, aligned west to east, with the head at the west end so that at the Resurrection the dead would sit up to face east. This was not always the case, however. Those who would not be resurrected – and this included unbaptised children, suicides and some criminals – were buried face down. Priests might be buried near the altar of their church, with their head at the east end, so that they would be facing their congregation at the Resurrection.

Unlike pagan burials, Christian graves do not usually contain offerings or grave goods. Rings are sometimes found on fingers, however, and people granted papal bullas ① (a piece of parchment attached to a lead disc granted by the Vatican in recognition of charitable deeds which would reduce the

Above An archaeologist cleaning a 'bier', used to transport and then lower bodies into graves. Small holes around the edges held the cords used to tie the body to the bier

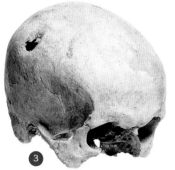

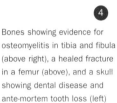

Above A skull from the medieval burial ground at Spitalfields. The two holes cut into it (only one visible here), indicate that it had been trepanned, a surgical practice thought to be a cure for epilepsy – the man survived the operation

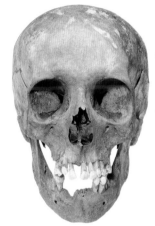

Bones showing evidence for osteomyelitis in tibia and fibula (above right), a healed fracture in a femur (above), and a skull showing dental disease and ante-mortem tooth loss (left)

number of years the owner's soul had to spend in purgatory) would be buried with them, placed on the chest or held in the hand. Priests were often buried with a pewter chalice and paten ❷ – their communion set – and a bishop might be buried with his staff. More commonly, people were buried with purses or bags of coins.

The dead were often placed in wooden coffins, although these are only preserved in favourable conditions, usually when the ground is waterlogged. Such coffins were often jointed or pegged together, with metal nails used to fix the lid on. Many people were simply buried in a shroud and all that survives of this is the pin which held the cloth together. Buckles and other fastenings sometimes survive to give a clue to the clothes the dead person was wearing when buried.

The richest members of society could afford to be buried in more elaborate ways. These included lead coffins and, more grandly still, tombs built of stone or brick which would once have had a carved lid, possibly bearing an inscription. Sometimes the body was buried inside the tomb, while in other cases the monument was built on top of the grave later. The very wealthy had their tombs in important churches and these were often beautifully carved, making a clear visual statement about the person's status.

Not surprisingly, the average age at death of medieval people was much lower than it is today, with many fewer children surviving into adulthood. This sad statistic is reflected in the large number of young children and babies found, as well as occasional unborn foetuses. Assessing the age of the skeletons of adults can be

difficult, but many clearly belonged to older men and women, particularly those who were wealthier and could afford a better diet. Specialists can analyse these skeletons to study diseases such as arthritis which tend to afflict older people.

It is rare that we can be confident of the cause of death from a skeleton, as in most cases only the organs, which do not survive, would have been affected. Sometimes, however, the cause is obvious – such as skeletons which still bear the marks of serious wounds caused by weapons or accidents. ❸ Diseases which affect the bones, such as tuberculosis or leprosy, also leave recognisable signs, though we still cannot be certain that the disease killed the individual. Instances are also known of people being badly crippled by accidents or disease. ❹

Right A medieval skeleton buried adjacent to a stake and wattle fence at Spitalfields

Right A burial in the Holy Trinity Priory graveyard

The largest assemblage of medieval skeletons excavated by archaeologists – over 10,000 **1** – comes from the Priory and Hospital of St Mary Spital. **2** They included all members of the monastic community, from the canons and priors who ran the monastery, to the lay sisters who looked after the sick, to the benefactors of the establishment, as well as the sick themselves. Many other of London's monastic houses have been excavated, for instance St Mary Graces at Tower Hill, Bermondsey Abbey, Merton Priory and Stratford Langthorne Abbey. Some of these cemeteries contained large numbers of skeletons, again including members of the of the monastic community as well as lay folk from the surrounding area.

Parish cemeteries are excavated less frequently as they are often still in use. Two good examples that have been are St Nicholas Shambles and St Benet Sherehog in the City. The burials at St Benet's **3** mostly dated from the post-medieval period, but the 234 burials at St Nicholas' were medieval. At St Nicholas' a variety of different burial practices were recorded, including 'charcoal burials', with the body laid on a bed of charcoal, burials laid on mortar, burials with stone pillows, **4** and cist burials. Cist burials are found in many Christian cemeteries and are thought to indicate relatively wealthy individuals. They usually consist of a stone coffin with a niche for the head. **5**

⑥ **Above** This grave slab marked the burial near St Paul's of a powerful Dane from around the time of Cnut (*c.* 1035); **Below** A Purbeck marble grave headstone recovered from St Benet's and dating from the 12th/13th century. The inscription says 'Here lies in the tomb Alice the wife of Peter'

Graves in a parish or monastic cemetery were only very rarely marked, ⑥ and while burials were probably laid out in neat rows initially, their exact location would soon be forgotten. As a result, and because of the large numbers of people buried in a relatively small area, graves in medieval cemeteries were constantly being disturbed by later burials. The older bones were collected and stored in specially built charnel houses. St Mary Spital's charnel house survived remarkably well ⑦ – the crypt was used for storing the bones ⑧ while above was once a chapel where services were held to say prayers for the souls of those whose bones had been disturbed.

Occasionally the dead were buried in mass graves, presumably at times of epidemics. Not only were there large numbers to bury but the gravediggers were perhaps afraid of the disease that had killed the dead and were keen to dispose of them as quickly as possible. Large pits were dug in the latter part of the thirteenth century at St Mary Spital, and thousands of people were interred in them. ⑨ The most dramatic discovery, however, was the Black Death cemetery at East Smithfield, where hundreds of bodies were buried in individual trenches. ⑩

Above The cemetery at Broad Street;
Right Burials in lead coffins

Above A 19th-century child burial from Southwark with the remains of a shroud and a pair of knitted booties

Post-medieval burial practices

As London's population expanded separate
cemeteries were created to accommodate the dead.

Above Analysis of skeletons from post-medieval burial grounds gives us a window on the lives as well as deaths of some of London's population; **Right** The brick burial vault at Farringdon Street after excavation

Archaeological evidence for cemetery use and burial practice in the years immediately following the Reformation in the 1530s reveals few changes, though an important new phenomenon occurs. This is the cemetery which is not attached to a church but is simply a plot of land used for Christian burial. The first of these, dating to the late sixteenth century, was the new cemetery on the site where Broad Street Station was later built, immediately to the north of the City walls. These new cemeteries must have been desperately needed as the space available for burial had been drastically reduced by the closure of London's monasteries. Archaeologists have excavated many hundreds of burials at the Broad Street cemetery, including some interred in mass burial pits. **1**

Parishes also built overflow cemeteries, such as at Farringdon Street **2** and the Cross Bones burial ground at Redcross Way in Southwark, which have both been excavated. The density of burials in these cemeteries was often very high, and they

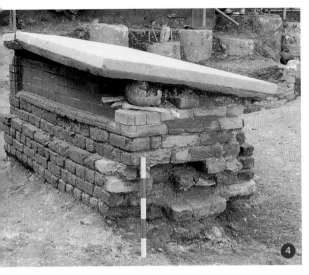

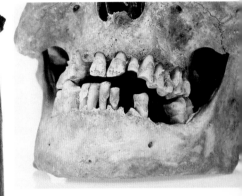

Above Teeth can provide evidence of the health and age of an individual. The wear on the teeth in this skull has been caused by the frequent gripping of a clay pipe stem whilst smoking; **Below** Recording the lead coffin of Mrs Lucy Orton, who died in her 35th year on 16 February 1898, from the crypt of St Lawrence Jewry. Archaeologists wear full protective clothing whilst recording lead coffins in a confined area

reflect the status and wealth of the parishioners. In many of the relatively recent interments the preservation of the coffins is good, and sometimes even clothing, hair or soft tissue survives. One typical burial practice was to dig a deep shaft in which coffins were stacked one on top of another as many as ten deep; another method was to excavate a large pit in which six or more coffins were placed at the base, and then others on top. The skeletons from Redcross Way reflect the poverty of the local inhabitants and documentary evidence suggests that this burial ground was used for the interment of prostitutes. Analysis of the skeletons has shown that over two-thirds belonged to children under the age of five – a graphic illustration of the high mortality rate at the time and in this particular area. ❸

The cemetery at St Benet Sherehog in the City continued as an overflow cemetery for St Stephen Walbrook after the Great Fire of 1666 had destroyed the church itself, which was not rebuilt. Two brick tombs were built in the cemetery – one housing the remains of Michael Davison and the other Mayor John Maurois, who died in 1673. ❹ In general, the cemetery was used for the poor of the parish and about 200 burials were found, mostly in coffins with decorated metal plates inscribed with the name of the deceased. ❺ Sometimes the coffins were so shallow that the nails used to fasten down the lid had penetrated the limbs of the corpse. ❻

Burials have also been found in wealthier areas, in particular in crypts, such as those at Christchurch Spitalfields and St Lawrence Jewry. A vault at the latter contained sixty burials in lead coffins, ❼ some elaborately decorated. These belonged to a wealthy parish in the City of London and dated between 1819 and 1845. Documentary evidence showed that most of the people had lived around the area of the church and were mainly from the families of merchants, particularly those involved in the clothing industries. As elsewhere, nearly half the burials were of children under the age of ten.

Disasters

London, like most cities, has been subject to many disasters throughout its history. Diseases like the plague killed many of its inhabitants and fires and wars destroyed their homes and often took their lives. Being sited on a river, London has also been flooded on many occasions from the prehistoric period right up to recent times. It is only the modern river defences that save Londoners from this threat today.

Above Burnt wooden beads had been spilt across the scorched brickearth floor of a Roman roadside shop at Poultry; **Right** The wooden beads after conservation

Fire

Of all the disasters which might befall us, fire is perhaps the commonest and is something all our ancestors had to face, particularly in such a crowded urban environment as London.

Recording the remains of a building destroyed by fire at Borough High Street, Southwark

London's fires have usually been local, confined perhaps to a single house or street, but on at least three occasions in the past large parts of the walled City have been consumed by flames.

The two earliest instances occurred during the first and second centuries AD. In AD 60 Boudica (often, though mistakenly, known as Boadicea) led her tribe the Iceni from East Anglia in rebellion against the Roman invaders. After overwhelming Colchester, Boudica and her followers attacked and burnt London, killing the inhabitants and destroying their homes and belongings. ❶ London was easy prey as it was then a trading settlement, undefended by walls or troops.

Fire debris found by archaeologists at many sites in the Roman city is evidence of the ferocity of the attack and the almost total destruction of the early settlement. ❷ This debris is even found on the southern side of the river, in Southwark, demonstrating

Above left Contemporary view of the Great Fire of 1666 by an unknown Dutch artist; **Above right** Hollar's engraving showing the effect of the Great Fire. Within the area shown white only the remains of a few of the more substantial stone buildings and churches still stood

Above The charred remains of wooden barrels lying on the cellar floor of a building in Pudding Lane destroyed in the Great Fire; **Below** An eyewitness' portrayal of a huge fire which broke out in Cotton's Depot Wharf in Southwark on Saturday 22 June 1861, visible 30 miles away

that Boudica's forces crossed the Thames in their desire to destroy the whole town.

About 60 years later, during the reign of the Emperor Hadrian, there was another major fire in the city, though this is more likely to have been accidental rather than the result of a deliberate attack. This fire too has left its mark on many sites, with thick deposits of ash and charcoal covering the destroyed buildings. Once again, the conflagration spread all the more easily because of the number of timber buildings in the city, and doubtless caused great loss of life.

London's most famous fire is of course that of 1666, which began in a baker's shop in Pudding Lane and spread so quickly and so fiercely that almost the entire walled city was destroyed. ③ The fire raged unchecked for days, and only the destruction of buildings in front of the Tower of London to create a fire gap prevented the gunpowder stores there being set alight

and exploding. Almost all of London's churches, including St Paul's Cathedral, were destroyed, and thousands of people were left homeless. Fortunately, and quite remarkably, there were very few fatalities, though we do not know how many died through lack of food, disease or injury in the aftermath.

Dry weather and the wind fanned the flames, but it was the timber houses built so close together that allowed the fire to leap from one side of the street to the other so easily. A thick horizon of ash and charcoal, like that resulting from the Roman fires, can still be seen at sites undisturbed by later building.

Archaeologists also regularly uncover individual buildings destroyed by fire. Charcoal and ash cover the former floors, and burnt posts are often all that remain to mark a disaster in someone's life, when their property and possessions were destroyed and perhaps their family killed.

Left Some of the many pins found at the Black Death cemetery at East Smithfield; many still retain remains of the burial shrouds which they fastened; **Above** Medieval 'Long Cross' coins from the cemetery; **Right** The rows of individual graves at the Black Death cemetery

Disease

The eradication of major epidemic diseases that once threatened the lives of huge numbers of London's population is a relatively recent phenomenon.

'The silent highwayman', a cartoon by Tenniel, illustrating the appalling state of the Thames in 1858

Various epidemics have affected Londoners, usually striking the most densely populated areas. Our knowledge of these diseases comes from documentary records and sometimes from the analysis of skeletons excavated by archaeologists from London's cemeteries.

The most notorious and probably the most lethal of all the epidemic diseases to afflict London was bubonic plague. It struck many times but most famously on two occasions. In 1348 the Black Death reached England at Melcombe Regis (now part of Weymouth) after ravaging mainland Europe. It is estimated that perhaps one- third of the population of London died in 1348–49 when the disease arrived in the city.

Initially the dead were buried in the parish cemeteries as usual, but as numbers rose rapidly this soon became impractical. Three emergency cemeteries were provided by

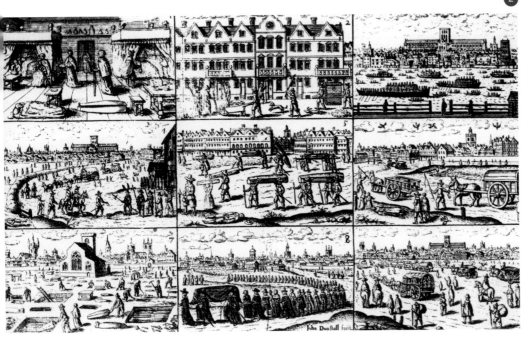

Parishes Names	1625.		1636.		1665.	
	Bu.	Pl.	Bu.	Pl.	Bu.	Pl.
Albans Woodstr.	188	78	42	13	200	121
Alhallows Bark.	397	263	142	32	514	330
Alhallows Breadstr.	34	14	14	2	35	16
Alhallows the Great	442	302	123	42	455	426
Alhallows Honylane	18	8	3	0	10	
Alhallows the lesse	259	205	47	8	239	175
Alhallows Lumb. ftr.	86	44	22	2	90	62
Alhallows Stayning	183	138	28	5	185	112
Alhallows the Wall	301	155	111	40	500	356
Alphage	240	150	62	11	271	115
Andrew Hubbard	146	101	26	10	71	7
Andrew Und. shaft	219	149	44	11	274	18
Andrew Wardrope	373	191	120	44	476	30
Ann Aldersgate	196	128	104	68	282	197
Ann Blackfryers	336	215	153	59	652	467
Antholins Parish	62	31	24	7	58	8
... Parish	72	40	20	2	43	2
Barthol. Exch.			19	0	73	2
Bennet Fynk	108	57	25	7	47	2
Bennet Gr. Church	48	14	16	1	57	4
Bennet Paulfwharf	216	131	112	49	355	17
Bennet Sherehog	24	8	9	0	11	
Botolph Billingfg.	99	66	30	9	83	7
Chrift Church	611	371	183	70	653	46
Chriftophers	48	28	13	6	60	4
Clement Eaftcheap	87	72	18	3	38	2
Dion's Back Chu.	99	59	17	2	78	2
Dunftans Eaft	335	225	64	8	265	15
Edm. Lumbard ftr.	78	49	15	2	70	1
G hereagh	205	101	61	27	195	10
Faiths	89	45	33	12	104	7
Fofters	149	102	40	7	141	10

Above Gruesome visual depiction of the time of a plague epidemic; **Above right** A plague broadsheet, being 'a true Account of how many persons died Weekly . . . and the Greatness of the Calamity and the Violence of the Distemper in the Last Year 1665'; **Right** The black rat, carrier of the fleas which bore the plague

wealthy citizens to dispose of the piles of corpses. Two were north-west of the city, where the Charterhouse was later built, and the third lay to the east of the city on Tower Hill, where the Abbey of St Mary Graces was subsequently founded. When archaeologists excavated this site, ① they found many individual graves alongside two long trenches in which skeletons were piled in layers five deep. About 1000 burials were excavated and estimates suggest that a total of about 2500 were originally interred there. Although buried in mass burial trenches, the skeletons were laid out in the traditional Christian manner with their heads at the west end and feet to the east, showing that despite the horrors of the time people were still buried with dignity and respect.

How many people died during the Black Death? It is difficult to say since we have not excavated all the skeletons from the burial grounds, many have been disturbed and numerous victims were buried in the parish cemeteries. Various estimates have been made of London's population at this time, ranging from 50,000 to 100,000. If a third of the population succumbed, then perhaps as many as 20,000 to 30,000 died at this time.

The second famous outbreak of bubonic plague was in 1665, when many thousands more died. ② Again parish cemeteries were used for the dead and emergency burial grounds were also provided, though these were smaller and much more numerous. None of these has been excavated but there was probably one for each district.

Smaller mass burial pits are also known, presumably to cope with outbreaks of disease at other times. Archaeologists have found large numbers dating from around 1300 at the Hospital of St Mary Spital and at the sixteenth-century New Cemetery beneath the old Broad Street Station.

London has been prey to numerous other epidemics, the most recent and lethal of which was the outbreak of cholera in the middle of the nineteenth century. The massive overcrowding and appalling sanitation in London ③ assisted its spread, and it was the catalyst for the building of London's sewers soon afterwards, which finally solved this threat to the health of Londoners.

Above London's first battle, when Caesar's invading army clashed with native warriors on the banks of the Thames in 54 BC

War

Conflict and wars have played a great part in shaping the city of London and the lives of its inhabitants.

The skull of a man with three separate wounds from a sharp–edged instrument like a sword or an axe

2 The Viking destruction of wooden London Bridge

London, as a capital city, has always been a major prize for armies throughout its history. Boudica sacked the town in AD 60 during her revolt against the Roman occupation of Britain, 1 and Viking raids in the ninth century focused on the city. 2 A small battle was fought over the capital in 1066 when the invading armies of William the Conqueror, having defeated Harold II at Hastings, were confronted by the people of London. It is not certain exactly where the battle took place, though it perhaps was on the west side of the city – skeletons laid on the foreshore by the River Fleet, excavated in the 1980s, may have been some of the casualties.

Some of the many thousands of skeletons excavated in London tell a personal tale of conflict, whether it was part of a large battle or a dispute between two individuals. Axe and sword wounds to the head, arms and legs graphically demonstrate the force of medieval weapons and the damage that they could inflict. Many of the injuries seen would undoubtedly have proved fatal, while others would have caused death

PETER JACKSON

later on through blood loss or septicaemia, given the poor level of medical knowledge of the times.

Another major battle fought in the London region took place at Barnet in north London in 1471, during the Wars of the Roses between the royal houses of York and Lancaster, though the site has never been archaeologically investigated. One famous fatality here was the Earl of Warwick – 'the Kingmaker'.

War affected the lives of Londoners twice in the course of the twentieth century. During the First World War a few buildings were destroyed by bombs dropped from Zeppelins, but the Second World War saw widespread destruction. ❸ Bombing left thousands dead and wounded and many more homeless, as well as causing massive damage to the architectural heritage of London. One attack destroyed Bank Underground Station and resulted in many casualties in the ticket hall. ❹ The devastation of the central part of London did, however, allow unprecedented archaeological investigation in the years

after the war by Professor W. F. Grimes and others.

Graphic evidence of the attacks during the Second World War was also found at the site of Low Hall Manor House in Walthamstow, on the eastern side of the River Lea. By the nineteenth century this manor house had already declined to the status of a farmhouse, but it was completely destroyed by a flying (V1) bomb in August 1944. The remains of the bomb and its crater were found in the courtyard in front of the house, ❺ a sad end to the 600-year history of the manor house.

More recent was the destruction of one of the few surviving medieval churches in the City of London, St Ethelburga's, which was blown up by a bomb planted by the IRA in 1996. ❻ This was a particular loss to the medieval fabric of London as so little had survived the previous devastation caused by both the Great Fire of 1666 and the Blitz of the 1940s.

Archaeologists reassemble timbers from the medieval belfry at St Ethelburga's

The future

Far left Advanced surveying techniques in use at Spitalfields; **Left** New scientific techniques such as DNA analysis are becoming available to archaeologists; **Above** Fragments of birds eggs can be identified by scanning electron micrographs, and it is possible to determine whether birds were kept for breeding or if wild resources were being exploited. This example shows a puffin egg, found at St Mary Spital

The future for London's archaeology

Advances in technology will help archaeologists to record, understand and preserve the past in the future. The future may also see more interpretation of our past disseminated by books, museums, the media and publically-accessible archives.

An old reconstruction of the Roman Governor's Palace found at Cannon Street. New excavations and re-interpretation of the old sites have led archaeologists to no longer believe that this is the 'Governor's Palace'

Technological advances are making huge differences to modern archaeology. Digital photographs and plans allow greater accuracy and quicker, more efficient recording. High-quality surveying techniques are now commonplace and the relationship between different sites can now be mapped much more precisely, while laser technology can record the details of tall, inaccessible buildings. When these technologies are combined with photographs and powerful computer software, demolished buildings and dismantled stonework can be reconstructed in two and three dimensions, creating a much more vivid 'feel' of the past.

Geographic information systems allow us to study ancient settlements in a way that could never even have been attempted before. The relevant information can be stored and we can then ask complex questions about artefacts, buildings, environment, lifestyle and landscape and

how they are interrelated, building up a picture of the development of an entire area. All aspects of the material relating to the Middle Saxon settlement of Lundenwic have been treated in this way, showing what can be achieved.

Archaeology in Britain has seen an increasing move towards studying archaeological remains without actually excavating them, thus preserving them for the future. Equipment which can look beneath the ground without disturbing it is therefore all the more vital, and a wide variety of these techniques have been developed over a number of years, the most recent of which is ground-penetrating radar. All these geophysical methods have their limitations – in particular problems are encountered with deep deposits which are commonly associated with urban sites, such as London, where occupation has taken place over such a long time. The time

when archaeologists no longer need to dig at all is still a long way off, but they now have many more tools at their disposal than just a trowel.

Perhaps the most significant development is the recognition by archaeologists that they need to make their findings and interpretations more accessible to a wider public. This is being achieved through museum displays and the presentation of monuments and of archaeological sites while they are under excavation. Vast amounts of archaeological information are now stored in boxes, on plans, photographs and in paper records, and making this information available to everyone is a Herculean task. One important innovation is the London Archaeological Archive and Research Centre in Hackney, where London's archaeological finds and data are stored and open to anyone who wishes to come and look at them.

As more sites are excavated and studied, and more information is analysed and interpreted, we are certain to uncover many more of London's archaeological secrets.

Found late in 2002 in Southwark, this stone plaque is the earliest known physical proof of London's Roman name (LONDINIENSIUM, on the 7th and 8th lines), dating to about AD 150

149

Where to visit

It is possible to visit some places of archaeological interest in London, as well as museums containing some of the artefacts found.

City

Museum of London, 150 London Wall

The Museum of London is the largest city museum in the world, telling the fascinating story of London from prehistoric times to the present day. It has eight main galleries of permanent exhibitions, and the most recent gallery – London Before London — focuses on the prehistory of the Thames Valley.
www.museumoflondon.org.uk

Tower of London, Tower Hill

The Tower of London is one of the world's most famous fortresses and has, since its construction in the 11th century, featured prominently in the history of Britain and the world. This designated World Heritage Site has served as a royal palace, a jail and a place of execution and its well-preserved buildings are of outstanding architectural significance.
www.hrp.org.uk/webcode/tower_home.asp

Billingsgate Bath House, 100 Lower Thames Street

Billingsgate Bath House is a well-preserved part of a Roman building in the City, forming one of the few substantial Roman remains in London. Visits can be arranged via the Museum of London.

Roman amphitheatre, Guildhall

The amphitheatre, built almost 2000 years ago, has been restored by the Corporation of London, and is situated beneath the Guildhall Art Gallery.
www.cityoflondon.gov.uk

The Guildhall

The Guildhall survives largely in its ancient form with most of the exterior masonry – stone towers, walls and crypts – dating from the 15th century.
www.cityoflondon.gov.uk

St Paul's

A Christian cathedral dedicated to St Paul was originally built on the site in AD 604, but the modern-day structure is the design of Sir Christopher Wren (who is buried in the Crypt), begun in the 17th century following the Great Fire of London.
www.stpauls.co.uk

Temple of Mithras

Discovered in 1954 on a large bomb site, the Roman Temple of Mithras can now be found at Temple Court, Queen Victoria Street, following relocation. Finds from the site – including the marble 'head of Mithras' – are housed in the Museum of London.

Bank of England museum

This Museum is housed within the Bank of England, and traces the history of the Bank from its foundation in the 17th century to its modern role in the heart of London's commercial centre. It houses archaeological finds including a Roman mosaic pavement, probably 4th-century, discovered during the interwar rebuilding of the Bank.
www.bankofengland.co.uk

Roman City Wall

The City square mile was originally bounded by a wall,and although this is no longer present in its entirety, substantial remains can be seen at the Barbican, by the Museum of London on the road names 'London Wall' and at Tower Hill. London streetnames ending in –gate also provide clues as to where the wall originally stood, and the Old Bailey (the Central Criminal Court in England) formerly stood in an ancient bailey of the city wall.

Sir John Soane Museum, Lincoln's Inn Fields

The museum was the 18th century home of Sir John Soane, and the design of the house reflects his desire to exhibit his collection of antiquities and works of art. Free to the public, the museum houses a large and diverse collection of artefacts.
www.soane.org

Lincoln's Inn

Lincoln's Inn is situated in the heart of London just off Chancery Lane and, with records stretching back as early as 1422, is the oldest of the four Inns of Court.
www.lincolnsinn.org.uk

Somerset House

Somerset House was the site of a Tudor palace and ornamental garden, which was pre-dated by various churches, chapels and cloisters. It now houses a permanent display of the fragments of the Tudor and Stuart royal palace discovered during excavations in 1997.
www.somerset-house.org.uk

Smithfield Market, Charterhouse Street

Meat has been bought and sold at Smithfield for over 800 years and a livestock market occupied the site as early as the 10th century. Although this makes it one of the oldest markets in London, Smithfield is one of the most modern meat markets in Europe, having recently undergone a £70 million refurbishment.
www.cityoflondon.gov.uk/our_services/markets

Greenwich

The Royal Park, Maritime Greenwich

The Royal Park in Maritime Greenwich – a designated World Heritage Site – dates from 1433, was modified in the 1660s, and still retains many of the original features and trees from that date. The Royal Observatory lies within the park.

www.royalparks.gov.uk

www.rog.nmm.ac.uk (for the observatory)

Hackney

Sutton House, Homerton High Street, Hackney

Sutton House in London's East End provides a fine example of a Tudor house. The building retains many original elements and has an exhibition explaining the history of the house. The property is managed by The National Trust.

www.nationaltrust.org.uk/regions/thameschilterns/

Hackney Museum, Reading Lane

The Hackney museum charts the history of the borough over the last 1000 years, with state of the art displays, education room and artefact stores. The Clapton Logboat, a well-preserved Saxon boat discovered in 1987 is on public display in the museum.

www.hackney.gov.uk/hackneymuseum

Haringey

Bruce Castle Museum, Lordship Lane, Haringey

Bruce Castle is a Grade I listed 16th-century manor house set in a large area of parkland. Some of the original parts of the building remain but the structure has been greatly modified over the centuries. The museum includes material from the Highgate Roman pottery kilns.

http://www.haringey.gov.uk/data/brucecastle

Islington

St Johns Gatehouse, Clerkenwell

The remains of the Priory of the Knights Hospitallers include a Tudor gatehouse, a 16th-century church and a 12th-century crypt.

The museum houses a large collection, with illuminated manuscripts and armour.

www.sja.org.uk/history

British Museum

The British Museum houses several collections which trace the story of Britain from prehistory to the present day, and holds lectures, courses and study days for those interested in learning more.

www.thebritishmuseum.ac.uk

Southwark

Rose Theatre

Remains of the Rose were discovered in 1988–9, but they were covered once excavations were complete, and are therefore not themselves visible but an exhibition can be viewed at Park Street.

New Globe Theatre

The Globe was built in 1599 and became the leading theatre of the day. A reconstructed Globe was opened in 1997, built with traditional materials and methods and the architects also drew on archaeological discoveries made at the site in 1989.

www.shakespeares-globe.org

Southwark Cathedral

The Cathedral is situated in the heart of Southwark on London's South Bank. It was built between 1220 and 1420, and has undergone major regeneration for the millennium. This includes the creation of a new exhibition – 'The Long View of London', which traces the history of Southwark through the centuries.

Winchester Palace, Clink Street

Part of the stone-built Great Hall of the residence of the Bishops of Winchester is still visible and the remains on display include the 14th-century Rose Window.

Platform Wharf, Rotherhithe and Edward III's manor

An information panel can be seen on the site of Edward III's manor house, later substantially altered to become part of Southwark's Delftware pottery industry.

Westminster

Westminster Abbey, Parliament Square

Westminster Abbey is an imposing architectural masterpiece, constructed over several centuries. The Abbey has been the setting for every royal coronation since the year 1066 and has played a central role in the country's history.

www.westminster-abbey.org

Palace of Westminster, Jewel Tower, Abingdon Street

From the mid 11th century until the fire of 1512, the Palace of Westminster was the principal residence of the kings of England. The Jewel Tower was built around 1365 at the request of Edward III, whose personal treasures it held.

www.parliament.uk

www.english-heritage.co.uk (Places to visit & events)

Lambeth Palace

Situated opposite the Palace of Westminster, Lambeth Palace has been the residence of the Archbishop of Canterbury for the past 900 years. It has a complex of buildings and extensive grounds as well as housing one of Britain's oldest public libraries.

www.archbishopofcanterbury.org/palace

The Banqueting House, Whitehall Palace

Designed by Inigo Jones, this is the only remaining complete building of Whitehall Palace where Charles I was executed in 1649.

www.hrp.org.uk

The Guildhall Art Gallery, with part of the outline of the amphitheatre, marked out on the courtyard surface, visible on the right

Glossary

barge bed – platform for barges at low tide

barrows – prehistoric burial mounds

basilica – Roman public hall

brickearth – a locally available glacial silt/clay deposit extensively used as a building material

cesspit – pit or chamber, sometimes lined with timber or stone, to hold human waste. The fills of cesspits often contain discarded pottery and other materials which can provide information about the occupants of a building

charnel house – building for older burials displaced by more recent ones

copper alloy – copper mixed with tin or other metal and used in the manufacture of jewellery, utensils and a variety of other objects

corbel – stone projecting from a wall to support weight

crenellations – battlements

Dissolution – the closure of the monasteries by Henry VIII between 1535 and 1540 and subsequent sale of buildings and land to secular owners. The majority of monastic buildings were eventually demolished though some survived as parish churches or bishops' palaces

hollow-way – road or track used over a long period of time and worn lower than the surrounding ground surface

hypocaust – Roman underfloor heating system

in situ – archaeological remain found in its original position and not moved by human or natural agents

Londinium – the Roman name for London

Lundenwic – the Saxon name for London

mudbrick – sun-dried 'mudbrick' buildings

posthole – holes from rotted posts

radiocarbon-dated – a method of dating organic materials by measuring the amount of the radioactive isotope carbon-14 they contain. Traces of carbon-14 are absorbed by live organisms but the isotope decays after death and eventually is no longer present

revetment/revetted – retaining wall frequently constructed of timber along river banks

samian ware – an imported Roman tableware

terrace – row of houses

tesserae – small tiles used to make mosaics

tree-ring dating/analysis – the study of the pattern of annual growth rings of trees which can provide dates for timber objects or structures and information about ancient environments

tumulus – prehistoric burial mound

undercroft – crypt

wattle and daub – interlaced branches covered with clay or mud to form walls

Periods mentioned in the text:

prehistoric – before the Roman period

Palaeolithic – approx 450,000–12,000 BC

Mesolithic – approx 12,000–4,000 BC

Neolithic – approx 4,000–2,000 BC

Bronze Age – approx 2,000–600 BC

Iron Age – approx 600 BC–43 AD

Roman – 43–410 AD

Saxon – 410–1066

medieval – 1066–1485

Tudor – 1485–1603

post-medieval – after the medieval period

Measurements are given in metric in this book:

m – metres (1 m = approx 3 feet 3 inches, 10 feet = approx 3 m)

km – kilometres (1 km = approx 1094 yards, 1 mile = approx 1.6 km)

Further reading

Peter Ackroyd, **London: the biography**, 2001

Nick Bateman, **Gladiators at the Guildhall: the story of London's Roman amphitheatre and medieval Guildhall**, 2000

Julian Bowsher, **The Rose Theatre: an archaeological discovery**, 1998

Penny Bruce and Simon Mason, **Merton Priory**, 1993

John Clark, **Saxon and Norman London**, 1989

Carrie Cowan, **Below Southwark – the archaeological story**, 2000

James Drummond-Murray, Chris Thomas and Jane Sidell, with Adrian Miles, **The big dig: archaeology and the Jubilee Line Extension**, 1998

Jenny Hall and Hedley Swain, **High Street Londinium: reconstructing Roman London**, 2000

Ian Haynes, Harvey Sheldon, and Lesley Hannigan, **London under ground: the archaeology of a city**, 2000

Peter Marsden, **Roman London**, 1980

Peter Marsden, **Ships of the port of London: first to the eleventh centuries AD**, 1994

Nick Merriman, **Prehistoric London**, 1990

Gustav Milne, **The Port of Roman London**, 1985

Gustav Milne, **Roman London**, 1995

Gustav Milne, **St Bride's Church London: archaeological research 1952–60 and 1992–5**, 1997

Museum of London Archaeology Service, **The archaeology of Greater London – an assessment of archaeological evidence for human presence in the area now covered by Greater London**, 2000

Dominic Perring, **Roman London**, 1991

Peter Rowsome, **Heart of the city: Roman, medieval and modern London revealed by archaeology at 1 Poultry**, 2000

David Saxby, **William Morris at Merton**, 1995

John Schofield, **Medieval London houses**, 1995

John Schofield with Cath Maloney (eds), **The Archaeological Gazetteer 1: Archaeology in the City of London 1907–91**, 1998

John D. Shepherd, **The Archaeological Gazetteer 3: Post-war archaeology in the City of London 1946–72**, 1998

Keith Sugden with Kieron Tyler, **Under Hackney – the archaeological story**, 2002

Christopher Thomas, **The archaeology of Medieval London**, 2002

Alan Thompson, Andrew Westman and Tony Dyson (eds), **The Archaeological Gazetteer 2: Archaeology in Greater London 1965–90**, 1998

Simon Thurley, **Whitehall Palace: an archaeological history of the royal lodgings 1230–1698**, 1999

Alan Vince, **Saxon London: an archaeological investigation**, 1990

Robin Wroe-Brown, **Bridging history: archaeology at the London Millennium Bridge**, 2000

Acknowledgements

The idea for this book was Peter Hinton and John Schofield's and thanks are also due to the City of London Archaeological Trust who generously helped to fund it. Peter Hinton acted as referee. The text is the result of may contributions from staff of the Museum of London Archaeological Services (MoLAS): Bruno Barber, Nick Bateman, Lyn Blackmore, Geoff Egan, Nick Elsden, Jackie Keilly, Peter Rowsome, Fiona Seeley, John Shepherd, Angela Wardle, Bruce Watson, Robin Wroe-Brown. The book was designed and typeset by Tracy Wellman. Picture research was by Andy Chopping and Tracy Wellman. The photographs were produced by MoLAS and Museum of London photographers, principally Andy Chopping, Maggie Cox, Edwin Baker, Torla Evans, John Chase, Richard Stroud, Jan Scrivener, Jon Bailey and Trevor Hurst. The maps were drawn by Jeanette van de Post, with other illustrations by Susan Banks, Sophie Lamb and Faith Vardy. The text was edited by Sarah Vernon Hunt.

The following institutions and individuals are thanked for their permission to reproduce illustrations on the pages indicated: Terry Ball, reproduced by permission of the Dean and Chapter of Westminster (90), Baltic Exchange Company (67), BBC's Meet the Ancestors (123), Martin Bentley (64), Chief Commissioner of the Metropolitan Police (48), Cross and Tibbs Collection, reproduced by permission of the Chief Commissioner of the Metropolitan Police (12, 143), Judith Dobie (25, 49, 66, 81, 84, 113, 130), Ronald Embleton (31, 34, 65), Peter Froste (18, 22, 24, 36, 48, 80), Frank Gardiner (19, 20, 30, 118), Chris Green (57), Guildhall Library, Corporation of London (10), Helen Jones (127), Derek Lucas (18, 19, 20, 21, 80, 96, 122, 142), Peter Jackson (32, 37, 83, 142), Museum of London / Andy Fulgoni (114), John Pearson (80), Kikar Singh (72, 83, 120, 127), Alan Sorrell (39, 48, 110, 113, 119, 146), Richard Sorrell (23, 60, 138), Dr Robert Spain (44), Uxbridge Local Studies and Archive (27), Faith Vardy (82). All other images are Museum of London Archaeology Service / Museum of London.

The top of the spire of Sir Christopher Wren's 17th-century church St Dunstan in the East, dwarfed and surrounded by today's office blocks. The continuing redevelopment of London allows archaeologists access to pockets of buried history, each one another piece in the jigsaw of London's archaeological secrets